Cambridge Elements ≡

Elements in Music and the City
edited by
Simon McVeigh
Goldsmiths, University of London
Laudan Nooshin
City, University of London

POPULAR MUSIC HERITAGE, CULTURAL JUSTICE AND THE DEINDUSTRIALISING CITY

Sarah Baker
Griffith University

Zelmarie Cantillon
Western Sydney University

Raphaël Nowak
University of York

CAMBRIDGE
UNIVERSITY PRESS

CAMBRIDGE
UNIVERSITY PRESS

Shaftesbury Road, Cambridge CB2 8EA, United Kingdom

One Liberty Plaza, 20th Floor, New York, NY 10006, USA

477 Williamstown Road, Port Melbourne, VIC 3207, Australia

314–321, 3rd Floor, Plot 3, Splendor Forum, Jasola District Centre,
New Delhi – 110025, India

103 Penang Road, #05–06/07, Visioncrest Commercial, Singapore 238467

Cambridge University Press is part of Cambridge University Press & Assessment,
a department of the University of Cambridge.

We share the University's mission to contribute to society through the pursuit of
education, learning and research at the highest international levels of excellence.

www.cambridge.org
Information on this title: www.cambridge.org/9781009066204

DOI: 10.1017/9781009067560

First published 2023

A catalogue record for this publication is available from the British Library.

ISBN 978-1-009-06620-4 Paperback
ISSN 2633-3880 (online)
ISSN 2633-3872 (print)

Popular Music Heritage, Cultural Justice and the Deindustrialising City

Elements in Music and the City

DOI: 10.1017/9781009067560
First published online: February 2023

Sarah Baker
Griffith University

Zelmarie Cantillon
Western Sydney University

Raphaël Nowak
University of York

Author for correspondence: Sarah Baker, s.baker@griffith.edu.au

Abstract: The celebration of popular music can be an important mode of cultural expression and a source of pride for urban communities. This Element analyses the capacity for popular music heritage to enact cultural justice in the deindustrialising cities of Wollongong, Australia; Detroit, USA; and Birmingham, UK. The Element develops a critical approach to cultural justice for examining music and the city in a heritage context and outlines how the quest for cultural justice manifests in three key ways: collection, preservation and archiving; curation, storytelling and heritage interpretation; and mobilising communities for collective action.

Keywords: cultural justice, popular music heritage, Wollongong, Detroit, Birmingham

ISBNs: 9781009066204 (PB), 9781009067560 (OC)
ISSNs: 2633-3880 (online), 2633-3872 (print)

Contents

1 Introduction

In the past several decades, industrial decline has contributed to substantial economic, social and cultural transformations for many local communities in Western countries. Beginning in the 1960s, the process of deindustrialisation refers to deep economic shifts relating to the delocalisation of manufacturing labour to cheaper markets (Bell, 1999). Historically, deindustrialising cities have faced significant problems with urban decay, unemployment and poverty. To combat the deleterious effects of deindustrialisation, many cities have looked to arts, culture and heritage for urban revitalisation and economic diversification. To this end, 'creative city' strategies have been adopted by many local governments seeking to attract investment in creative industries, expand a city's cultural offer, strengthen the service economy and reorient their urban identity (see Barnes et al., 2006; Goldberg-Miller, 2019; Waitt & Gibson, 2009). In some cases, such strategies have involved placing a significant emphasis on popular music to the extent that they brand themselves as 'music cities' (Ballico & Watson, 2020). This trend encompasses promoting contemporary live music scenes as well as looking to the past through popular music heritage initiatives.

Popular music heritage broadly refers to the preservation and celebration of places, materials, practices, events, memories and stories related to the production and consumption of popular music in the recent past. This Element explores the relationship between practices of popular music heritage and popular music's communities of interest in cities impacted by deindustrialisation. In particular, our attention is drawn to the potentials of popular music heritage to enact cultural justice by way of, for instance, showcasing the histories of socially marginalised groups, reworking cultural narratives around place and urban identity, conserving material remnants of heritage and bringing diverse groups together to advance understandings of popular music's past and its connections to the social, political, economic and cultural fabric of cities. Focusing on the deindustrialising cities of Birmingham (West Midlands, England), Detroit (Michigan, USA) and Wollongong (New South Wales, Australia), we explore examples of popular music heritage practice related to collection, preservation and archiving; curation, storytelling and heritage interpretation; and the mobilising of communities for collective action. Our analysis of popular music heritage initiatives reveals how they can variously *resist* and/ or *reinforce* cultural injustices in the deindustrialising city.

Popular music heritage discourse is conceptualised by Roberts and Cohen (2014) as situated on a continuum: unauthorised, self-authorised and officially authorised. Unauthorised popular music heritage initiatives often exist 'without even an awareness that [they *are*] heritage' (Roberts & Cohen, 2014, p. 257, original emphasis); their archiving is unintentional and the emphasis is on everyday practices and individual and collective memory. Self-authorised initiatives, on the other hand, are intentional in their heritage practice and make 'claims to (or solicitations of) some form of official status' in terms of their development, operations and sustainability (Roberts & Cohen, 2014, p. 248). These initiatives tend to be characterised by precarious funding and a do-it-yourself (DIY) ethos with an emphasis on 'localised or vernacular popular music heritage discourses' (Roberts & Cohen, 2014, p. 248). Officially authorised initiatives constitute 'big H' heritage in the sense that they have substantial funding streams and are sanctioned by government bodies, giving them a degree of legitimacy not afforded to self-authorised or unauthorised popular music heritage. In this Element, we look at a range of practices along the continuum, but especially self-authorised initiatives which take 'a DIY approach to heritage' (Baker, 2018). However, we acknowledge that heritage initiatives are not fixed in their discourse or practice but can move along the continuum in both directions. As such, the self-authorised initiatives we analyse also engage in partnerships with officially authorised institutions and connect with unauthorised heritage practice through the crowdsourcing of archival materials.

The target audience for this Element is heritage practitioners, as well as scholars of popular music, heritage studies and urban studies. While the focus is on popular music as a cultural form, with its setting being the deindustrialising city, the conceptual lens of cultural justice has broader relevance beyond these contexts. Consequently, the Element will be of interest to a wider audience than the title suggests. It is also important to note that the heritage initiatives we discuss are not intended to be exemplars of best practice for cultural justice; rather, they provide useful case studies for critically examining how the quest for cultural justice can unfold, to varying degrees of success and while facing obstacles. Analysing the case studies through a cultural justice lens offers valuable lessons in how more culturally just approaches to heritage can be undertaken in the future. In this opening section, we posit our contextual and conceptual framework to identify the potential for cultural justice within practices of popular music heritage. The section introduces the three case study cities, offering an overview of these in relation to processes of deindustrialisation and their credentials as places of interest in terms of popular music heritage. We then provide a brief outline of our research methods, introduce our key participants and reflect on researcher positionality. To begin, however, we explore some of the issues that have recently been noted about culture, which further highlights the need for the concept of cultural justice.

1.1 The Problem with Culture

In accounts of music audiences (e.g. DeNora, 2000; Hennion, 2007), music is understood as an instrument of self-realisation via mediating everyday experiences through embodied interactions. Such work implicitly poses music as inherently 'good', with its meaning constructed through the uses and affects of those who enjoy it. Such work disregards how music intersects with broader social forces and how its production, distribution and consumption is constrained by systemic inequalities. As Hesmondhalgh (2008, p. 330) suggests, scholarly work focused on individuals' listening practices presents an overly positive perspective on music that is 'somehow independent of negative social and historical processes'. For example, in their recent critical work, *Culture is bad for you*, Brook and colleagues (2020) highlight intensifying issues of inequality in the cultural industries, focusing their attention on access to and exclusion from cultural production based on class, race and gender. One of their key findings is the overreliance of cultural production on free labour and, therefore, on the exploitation of creative workers, especially those from working-class backgrounds (Brook et al., 2020). Such inequalities 'limit the potential value and impact of culture' (Brook et al., 2020, p. 44). Critical interventions by scholars like Hesmondhalgh (2008) and Brook and colleagues (2020) serve to reinscribe how culture is tied to structural economic and social conditions.

Heritage has also been framed in terms of its positive benefits on individuals and communities, having been linked to an increased sense of well-being and improved health outcomes (see Pennington et al., 2019). However, beyond the boosterist discourse, heritage can also be connected to experiences of distress and trauma. When heritage is threatened or damaged, or its value is not recognised and respected, then individual and community well-being can be negatively impacted (Taçon & Baker, 2019). An uncritical celebration of heritage – in policy, institutions and scholarship – can mask its capacity for reproducing suffering or injustice, as evident in work on heritage and decoloniality (Ghaddar & Caswell, 2019) and human rights (Logan, 2012). Looking specifically at popular music heritage, Fairchild (2021, p. 24) argues that museums are institutions that 'continue to be imbued with an aura of democratic optimism and empowerment'. Fairchild (2021, p. 224) rejects the notion that popular music museums' primary missions are to preserve, celebrate and educate about popular music's past, asserting that they may use vast amounts of 'public resources ... to serve the highly specific, private interests of the real estate and tourism industries'. He contends that readings of popular music as democratic ignore how its production and consumption are intrinsically located within ideological and hierarchical fields of power (Fairchild, 2021).

The critical lens of the scholars cited in the opening paragraphs of Section 1.1 contributes to contemporary debates about structural issues with cultural and music production and its effects on the social and cultural value of music. In doing so, their work is situated against a somewhat taken-for-granted notion that culture is 'good' and produces 'good effects'. While previous research accounts for some of the symptoms associated with contemporary cultural production and distribution, more clarity is needed as to the tools that musicians, heritage practitioners or cultural workers might deploy and develop to resist the reproduction of societal injustices through culture. We suggest that a concept such as cultural justice offers the potential to disrupt a flawed and unequal field of cultural production with possibilities for heritage practitioners, enthusiasts, musicians and listeners to intervene on, or even seize, the meaning of popular music by way of heritage *and* the meaning of local heritage by way of popular music. Put simply, we do not situate our perspective in relation to contemporary conversations about whether culture is 'good' or 'bad', or if heritage 'makes you happy' (Historic England, 2014). Instead, we acknowledge the structural issues related to cultural production and seek to conceptualise how the tools of cultural justice *potentially* empower different actors to address those issues in ways that might generate more positive outcomes from engaging in cultural practices broadly and heritage practices specifically. We approach this task with a critical eye, recognising that the quest for cultural justice is challenging and has the capacity to reinforce injustices or even introduce other forms of injustice.

1.2 Intersections of Justice and Heritage

Since the 2000s, there has been an observable 'justice turn' within heritage, museum and archival studies. This justice turn has been nurtured by work in critical heritage studies, community archives and new museology scholarship that addresses issues of power and inequality. Smith (2006) posits that institutional heritage practice in the West has long been shaped by an authorised heritage discourse which emphasises materiality, 'age, monumentality and/or aesthetics' (p. 3) in the assessment of heritage value and takes these qualities to be 'innate and immutable cultural values' (p. 4). Work in the field of heritage studies has questioned these assumptions, highlighting the intangibility, dynamism and constructedness of heritage – as a present interpretation or performance of the past – and drawing attention to the power relations that underpin it. These concerns are obvious in research on heritage and social change (Byrne, 2008; Chynoweth et al., 2021), activism (Flinn, 2011; Janes & Sandell, 2019), decoloniality (Ghaddar & Caswell, 2019; Vawda, 2019) and different forms of justice. We discuss concepts of social justice and cultural justice more in-depth in Sections 1.2 and 1.2.1, but it is also important to note the emergence and development of ideas such as restorative justice (Simpson, 2009), transitional justice (Burch-Brown, 2020) and heritage justice (Joy, 2020).

Most of the literature on the interface between heritage and justice focuses on *social* justice. Duff and colleagues (2013), writing on archives, outline that social justice can encompass the distribution of power and resources; issues of recognition, disrespect, marginalisation, participation, exclusion and repatriation; and resistance against systems of domination and inequality. Similarly, Punzalan and Caswell (2016, p. 27) note the importance of issues including 'Inclusion of underrepresented and marginalized sectors of society'; 'Development of community archives'; and 'Efforts to document human rights violations'. Baird (2014, p. 12) details other key questions underpinning the social justice approach: 'how is heritage mobilized in knowledge claims and identity creation? Are specific discourses or practices privileged in the name of safeguarding heritage? Are certain voices included and/or silenced?' In terms of how social justice values are reflected in heritage practice, the literature stresses the importance of public access and participation, addressing gaps or silences in collections, and taking community-led or collaborative approaches to documenting history (Baird, 2014; Duff et al., 2013; Johnston & Marwood, 2017; Punzalan & Caswell, 2016).

For heritage practitioners, there are ongoing challenges in attempting to embed social justice values within conventional collecting and preservation objectives (Witcomb & Buckley, 2013). For example, Janes and Sandell (2019, p. 8) observe that museum professionals face 'persistent anxiety' and structural constraints to pursuing activism and social justice, including institutional agendas that prioritise digitisation projects and audience development, as well as pressures to strive for neutrality and avoid 'alienat[ing] government and private funders'. These challenges mirror those discussed in Section 1.1 in relation to problems faced in the cultural industries more broadly.

1.2.1 Cultural Justice

While references to social justice are increasingly common in critical heritage studies and allied fields, engagements with the idea of *cultural* justice remain limited. We turn to scholarly work from other fields like critical theory, cultural history and critical cultural studies to address this absence. Cultural justice is borne out of the concept of social justice – it acknowledges issues of power and inequalities while introducing a broadly defined variable of 'culture' (Ross, 1998, p. 194). We propose that cultural justice 'offers a more precise lens through which to consider the cultural dimensions of injustice' (Cantillon et al., 2021a, p. 75). Cultural justice accounts for social inequalities that may be constructed or reproduced through culture – for example, the privileging of certain identities and narratives in cultural representations.

Fraser (1995, p. 71, emphasis added) defines cultural injustices as:

> rooted in social patterns of representation, interpretation, and communication. Examples include *cultural domination* (being subjected to patterns of interpretation and communication that are associated with another culture and are alien and/or hostile to one's own); *nonrecognition* (being rendered invisible via the authoritative representational, communicative, and interpretative practices of one's culture); and *disrespect* (being routinely maligned or disparaged in stereotypic public cultural representations and/or in everyday life interactions).

In the context of our research on deindustrialising cities, Fraser's (1995, p. 69) work is instructive in that it acknowledges how cultural domination, non-recognition and disrespect are inevitably 'entwined with' and supported by economic disadvantage. In Fraser's reckoning (1995, pp. 72–3), 'economic disadvantage impedes equal participation in the making of culture'. Although economic and cultural injustices are inter-implicated, they can be analytically separated in that 'the remedy for economic injustice is political-economic restructuring', captured by 'the generic term "redistribution"', while in the case of cultural injustice, the remedy is a form of cultural change captured by 'the generic term "recognition"' (Fraser, 1995, p. 73).

Ross (1998, p. 191) echoes Fraser in arguing that cultural justice is enmeshed in 'the transformation of socioeconomic conditions'. Writing on the impact of economic realities on cultural expressions, Ross (1998, p. 2) defines cultural justice as 'doing justice to culture, pursuing justice through cultural means, and seeking justice for cultural claims'. He argues that 'respectful recognition' of differences can provide 'material and ethical improvement of our lives' and subvert 'the channels of official neglect, economic subordination, and cultural denigration and turn them into routes toward pride, empowerment, and equity' (Ross, 1998, p. 3). Denning (2004, pp. 164–5) similarly emphasises 'politics of recognition', 'the battle over the relations of representation' and 'struggles to reassert the dignity of despised cultural identifications'. He speaks specifically of the heritage sector, noting that the 'struggle for cultural justice is also a struggle to reshape the selective traditions that determine which works of art and culture will be preserved, kept in print, taught to young people, and displayed in museums, and which cans of film will be housed, whose manuscripts and letters will be archived and indexed' (Denning, 2004, p. 165).

Denning (2004, pp. 164–5) argues that 'artists, intellectuals, and cultural workers' can 'self-organise and create organisations and cultural institutions that can work to reinstate dignity' and fight for 'equal access' to such institutions. Banks (2017) likewise refers to the importance of cultural workers in his work on creative justice. Drawing on Ross' work, Banks (2017, pp. 1–2) explores three kinds of justice relating to the cultural industries: paying respect to culture as something with 'objective' value; recognising the pluralistic value (economic, social, aesthetic) of cultural work; and attending to the uneven distribution of resources and opportunities on behalf of cultural institutions.

The scholarship cited in Section 1.2.1 offers valuable guidance as to some of the core principles of cultural justice, which we summarise elsewhere as 'the recognition and value of cultural objects, cultural institutions and cultural work, as well as issues of power, participation, access and representation' (Cantillon et al., 2021a, p. 75). How, then, does cultural justice manifest in practice? Banerjee and Steinberg (2015), writing on the use of culture in environmental activism, put forth three key tools that comprise a cultural justice toolkit:

1. *Symbologies of place* – material artefacts, landmarks and 'physical remains of a community's past history' as well as 'images of ongoing economic and cultural relationships in the community' and 'cultural symbols and imaginaries' (Banerjee & Steinberg, 2015, p. 43).
2. *Historiographies of space* – historical narratives and 'place-based storytelling' that 'promote and protect cultural ties that affirm collective cultural identities' (Banerjee & Steinberg, 2015, p. 43).
3. *Social ties and community networks* – bringing together communities for collective action through both informal, 'intra-community' initiatives and resources, such as 'financial support, volunteering, and organizational needs' (Banerjee & Steinberg, 2015, p. 44) and 'inter-community' support, such as 'relationships with well-established activist networks' that can help bolster their reach and visibility (Banerjee & Steinberg, 2015, p. 48).

The conceptual framework and structure of this Element is informed by Banerjee and Steinberg's toolkit. Building on their scholarship, we rework the aforementioned tools in the context of popular music heritage initiatives in deindustrialising cities. Importantly, we aim to bring a critical lens to cultural justice, examining the complexities of how popular music heritage may both *resist* injustices as well as *reproduce* them.

That cultural justice is an underutilised concept in critical heritage studies is surprising given that 'heritage is a *cultural* product (and process) that seeks to represent *cultural* identities, expressions, practices, symbols and materialities' (Cantillon et al., 2021a, pp. 74–5, original emphasis). The most substantive work on heritage and cultural justice stems from our own research – often in collaboration with Paul Long, Lauren Istvandity and Jez Collins – on popular music heritage (Cantillon et al., 2021a, 2021b; Long et al., 2017, 2019). The outputs by Long and colleagues (2017, 2019) focus primarily on community archives of popular music, using cultural justice to refer to processes by which we can do justice to culture – specifically, recognising the value of popular music history, which has often been trivialised within authorised heritage institutions and discourses. Drawing on Banerjee and Steinberg's (2015) toolkit, our most recent work explored the relationship of each of the three tools to examples of popular music heritage initiatives in deindustrialising cities (Cantillon et al., 2021a). In doing so, we reframed the tools of cultural justice as: (1) collection, preservation and archiving; (2) curation, storytelling and heritage interpretation; and (3) mobilising communities for collective action. In this Element, we extend our understanding of the application of a critical cultural justice lens by exploring the tools in relation to a varied array of popular music heritage practices in our case study cities of Detroit, Birmingham and Wollongong.

1.3 Introducing the Deindustrialising Cities of Our Study

Communities experiencing industrial decline have struggled with significant socio-economic injustices, including unemployment, urban decay, inadequate public services and infrastructure, increased poverty and higher crime rates (Doucet, 2020). These challenges intersect with and amplify existing inequalities, dispropor-tionately impacting people of colour, migrant populations and working-class groups (Shaw, 2000). Such social and economic injustices are subsequently implicated in cultural injustices, including stigmatisation, disrespect and derision of both place and people. The negative connotations attached to deindustrialising cities were acknowledged by our research participants. Wollongong has long been known as a 'dirty town' (Julie, 9 October 2018; Brian, 10 October 2018; John, 11 October 2018), a 'violent and run down sort of steel city' (Aaron, 9 October 2018) with 'a pretty big violence problem' (Ashley, 9 October 2018). Birmingham had 'gangs everywhere' (Bill, 3 September 2019), was 'very run-down, very dark, very depressive' (Mark, 2 September 2019) and 'was looked upon as this making place: cars, coal, concrete, boring middle of the country, nothing ever happened there, and our accents reflected that' (Jez, 1 April 2019). Detroit had become 'blighted', a 'tumbleweed' town, 'the world's poorest city' with the coun-try's 'highest crime rates' (Matt, 11 April 2019), driven by 'the drugs, the gangs, the crime syndicates' (Michelle, 8 April 2019). These narratives do not, of course, capture the social and cultural vitality and local distinctiveness that also constitute such places.

Popular music is perceived by many policymakers to be 'a potentially powerful driver for urban economic development and city-specific tourism' (Ballico & Watson, 2020, p. 1). The result of the 'economization of cultural policy' is that arts and culture are viewed instrumentally in terms of creativity being supported because it 'promotes innovation', which, in turn, 'promotes economic benefits' (Klamer et al., 2013, p. 37). However, this approach can be problematic. We noted in Section 1.1 that cultural and creative industries are not inherently positive, nor a panacea for social and economic problems. The uneven injustices faced by communities in deindustrialising cities have long-term structural impacts that continue to deepen even as these places undergo transformations. As Lawson (2020, p. 9) points out, 'deindustrialisation not only hallowed out working-class neighbourhoods but also exacerbated the racial and class inequalities that prevent the new wealth generated by creative industries from being shared widely across society'. While cultural policy aimed at urban regeneration can be implicated in the displacement of communities through gentrification (Çağlar & Schiller, 2018; Shaw & Porter, 2009), Grodach and colleagues (2018) indicate this is not always the case. It is crucial, therefore, to consider cultural policy, creative city strategies and popular music heritage initiatives through the lens of cultural justice – how can cultural expressions and industries be deployed to revitalise deindustrialising cities in a more *just* way?

Despite social, economic and environmental challenges, people in cities still find ways to produce vibrant cultural and creative works that respond to the urban experience. Popular music has been a core means of cultural expression for communities in deindustrialising cities; some of the most well-known popular music that has emerged from our case study cities is marked by its industrial roots. In Birmingham, Bottà (2015, p. 113) notes that bands like Black Sabbath and Judas Priest were influenced by the 'rhythm of the factory', while Harrison (2010, p. 145) observes the themes of these bands' lyrics reflect a 'poor, working-class experience'. Similarly, in Detroit, Che (2009, p. 261) argues that 'techno is tied to Detroit's automotive heritage and its high-wage opportunities under Fordism ... and to the city's subsequent deindustrialization'. Likewise, John Monteleone, director of the Wollongong Art Gallery (WAG), writes

> It is no coincidence that some of the most powerful music created over the past century has come out of working class towns and cities around the world. Cities and towns possess something like a soul – insubstantial vessels that contain the

essence of time, memory and community identity and spirit. Within these places it is the everyday struggles to survive, a general disenchantment with the state of society, as well as a discomfort with social prejudice and the disaffection it engenders that provide a perfect foundation for an explosion of a new creative energy. (Wollongong Art Gallery, 2014, p. 2)

These examples highlight some of the myriad ways in which cultural expressions are intertwined with and mediated by economic circumstances and upheavals. Of course, not all music being produced in (de)industrial(ising) cities sonically, lyrically or aesthetically reflects factory life.

Paying attention to the production and consumption of popular music in deindustrialising cities also complicates dominant narratives of place identity. As highlighted by our interview participants in the opening paragraph of Section 1.3, the deindustrialising city is often characterised as 'a victim or a place of loss' (Linkon & Russo, 2002, p. 246), closely associated with despair, pollution and crisis. Turning to past and present music cultures in these cities may underscore their 'robust social organization and community life' (Linkon & Russo, 2002, p. 246), cultural diversity and creative vibrancy. At the same time, looking to the past can acknowledge and make visible 'difficult heritage' (Macdonald, 2009), particularly in relation to experiences of trauma and oppression (see Cvetkovich, 2003). These possibilities point to the heterogeneous manifestations of cultural justice and injustice afforded by popular music heritage in the deindustrialising city.

The cities we focus on in this Element were selected as case studies based on several criteria. Firstly, each city had experienced rapid urban development and population growth throughout the early- to mid-twentieth century supported by strong manufacturing industries. Secondly, each experienced significant industrial decline followed by concerted urban revitalisation projects over the past several decades, representing a shift from Fordist manufacturing economies to post-Fordist, culture-led activities (Che, 2008). Thirdly, each city has a reputation for rich popular music histories and thriving contemporary music scenes, as well as the recent emergence of heritage initiatives that serve to document, protect and share this musical activity. Next, we provide a brief overview of each case study city's history in relation to deindustrialisation, urban renewal, popular music production and consumption, and related heritage initiatives.

1.3.1 Detroit

Detroit is a major city located in southeast Michigan near the Canada–US border. Described as the 'iconographic post-industrial legacy city' (Kinkead, 2016, p. 46), the ruins of Detroit's manufacturing plants are representative of the sheer scale of industrial decline and urban decay that unfolded beginning in the 1950s. In the early twentieth century, Detroit grew rapidly along with its thriving automobile manufacturing industry, becoming known as the 'Motor City'. Detroit's population has more than halved since the 1950s – peaking at 1.8 million in 1950 (Shaw, 2000), by 2021 the population had fallen to 634,000 (United States Census Bureau, 2021), representing the 'seventh straight decade' of population decline (Kozlowski, 2021). Multiple, complex factors have contributed to extreme population decline and urban shrinkage in Detroit, including the downsizing and disinvestment of manufacturing industries. Racial inequalities and tensions have also played a significant role, with suburbanisation exacerbating 'white flight' and spatial segregation in Detroit and surrounding areas (Fraser, 2018; Pedroni, 2011; Ryzewski, 2019). More recently, the city's residents – the majority of whom are Black – were severely impacted by the 2008–9 subprime mortgage crisis and resulting foreclosures (Rugh & Massey, 2010; Safransky, 2018). These issues, along with increases in poverty and decreases in property values and tax revenue (Sugrue, 1996; Wilson, 1992), contributed to numerous abandoned, decaying buildings and vacant lots spread across many neighbourhoods. The unemployment rate in Detroit peaked at more than 28 per cent in 2009 (Thibodeau & Noble, 2018) and the city filed for bankruptcy in 2013.

Detroit has been subject to multiple urban regeneration efforts. At the time of writing, the unemployment rate in Detroit was 4.8 per cent, with diversified major sectors of employment, including professional and business services; trade, transportation, and utilities; education and health services; manufacturing; leisure and hospitality; and financial services (United States Bureau of Labor Statistics, 2021). Changes in the city have been spurred by 'large-scale redevelopment, ruin tourism and entrepreneurialism' (Fraser, 2018, p. 443). As one notable example of entrepreneur-led gentrification, billionaire Dan Gilbert relocated the offices for his mortgage lending business Quicken Loans to downtown Detroit in 2010 and proceeded to purchase large swathes of real estate in the area (Eisinger, 2014). Just north of downtown, Midtown has solidified itself as the city's major cultural hub, home to numerous arts, heritage and knowledge institutions, including Wayne State University, Michigan Science Center, Detroit Institute of Arts, Detroit Historical Museum, Charles H Wright African American Museum and Orchestra Hall. In particular, Wayne State University is seen as an 'anchor institution' that has been key to revitalisation of the area (Briller & Sankar, 2013; Florida & Adler, 2018). In other nearby neighbourhoods such as Corktown, which has seen an uptick in art galleries, music venues and restaurants (Che, 2007), renewal has instead been spearheaded by 'residents, local businesses and volunteers'

(Doucet & Smit, 2016, p. 637). Of course, new economic activity and investment in Detroit has not been inherently beneficial. Doucet (2020) explores the racist and exclusionary nature of gentrification in Detroit, while Fraser (2018) observes that the renovation or demolition of urban ruins has displaced residents and erased some of the material reminders of the city's past. In this way, present-day 'blight removal' projects mirror devastating 'urban renewal' initiatives from the 1950s and 1960s, which saw the vibrant Black neighbourhood Black Bottom razed and replaced by the Chrysler Freeway (Feeley, 2016; see also Herstad, 2017). Thus, significant injustices are still embedded in attempts to bounce back following industrial decline.

Detroit has a rich musical history, known for jazz, blues, gospel, soul, techno, pop, rock and hip hop, including the artists of Motown, such as Diana Ross, and other renowned musicians like Aretha Franklin, Suzi Quatro, The White Stripes, Juan Atkins, Eminem and MC5 (see also Gholz, 2011). Detroit is home to both officially authorised popular music heritage institutions such as the Motown Museum and self-authorised activities like Exhibit 3000, an appointment-only techno museum. Heritage activities in the city are also spearheaded by non-profit organisations such as the Detroit Sound Conservancy (DSC), established in 2012 to '[e]nhance Detroiters' quality of life through preservation, education, performance, and placekeeping' projects focused on popular music history (Detroit Sound Conservancy, 2021b).

1.3.2 Birmingham

Birmingham is the urban centre of England's heavily industrialised West Midlands region. The second largest city in the United Kingdom, Birmingham's population has risen and fallen over the decades, but sits at about 1.1 million at the time of writing (Birmingham City Council, 2021). Described as 'The City of a Thousand Trades', Birmingham was the hub of England's industrial revolution and became known for its prosperous, diverse industrial economy (Hubbard, 1995; McEwan et al., 2008). As in many other industrialised cities, culturally diverse migrant communities were integral to Birmingham's workforce (Collins, 2015). By the mid-1900s, Birmingham had become increasingly specialised in automobile engineering and manufacturing. Towards the end of the 1970s and into the 1980s, the city experienced a sudden major economic collapse, with massive job losses and rapid urban decline, attributed in part to an over-dependence on its car manufacturing industry (Loftman & Nevin, 1994; Martin, 1995). From 1981 to 1991, 70,000 manufacturing jobs were lost, and unemployment peaked at 21 per cent in 1986 (Shaw, 2000). Similar to Detroit, Birmingham's industrial decline was coupled with 'outward migration of relatively affluent residents who, nevertheless, retained and commuted to jobs in the city ... This contributed to an erosion of the city's tax base without reducing significantly demand on Birmingham's public services and exacerbated the polarisation between inner city and suburbs' (Martin, 1995, p. 200).

Birmingham responded to its deindustrialisation by attempting to broaden the city's economic base, shifting towards service-based industries and striving to regenerate the CBD and the city's image (Hubbard, 1995; Loftman & Nevin, 1994; Martin, 1995). This regeneration was initially led by the local government, which later prompted greater private investment and public–private developments (Andres & Chapain, 2013). Over the past several decades, Birmingham has progressively been recovering, albeit with periods of fragility, particularly during the 2007–8 global financial crisis and its aftermath. The unemployment rate remains elevated compared to the national average at the time of writing – although it had been decreasing in the late 2010s (Birmingham City Council, 2019; Greater Birmingham Chambers of Commerce, 2018a), the onset of the COVID-19 pandemic saw unemployment rates soar to levels similar to the 1980s (Drury, 2021). Birmingham's key industries now include education, health and financial services (Greater Birmingham Chambers of Commerce, 2018b). Cultural industries have played a particularly important role in Birmingham's regeneration efforts (Andres & Chapain, 2013), with the Jewellery Quarter and Digbeth being the loci for creative activity. The CBD and surrounds have undergone substantial change, marked by flagship urban redevelopment projects such as the Broad Street Leisure Area and The Bullring shopping centre (Barber & Hall, 2008). In 2022, the city hosted the Commonwealth Games, offering another opportunity for urban regeneration and reimaging (see e.g. Cantillon, 2022). Much like Detroit, however, 'the socio-spatial impact of economic restructuring and the resulting policy response has been extremely uneven', with increasing disadvantage among 'inner city areas with large ethnic minority populations' (Barber & Hall, 2008, p. 281). In particular, problems arise when regeneration efforts are focused only on regenerating the material fabric of cities (Hubbard, 1995).

Birmingham's popular music reflects the city's diverse communities. Genres that have flourished in the city include reggae, heavy metal, bhangra, progressive rock, folk, punk, post-punk, techno, dub, grime and indie (Collins, 2020b). Many of Birmingham's bands and musicians – including Joan Armatrading, Steel Pulse, Christine McVie, Black Sabbath, UB40, Electric Light Orchestra, Duran Duran, The Streets and Editors – have found sustained international success. Popular music heritage initiatives currently active in the city include the Birmingham Music Archive (BMA), an online archive and community heritage organisation founded by Jez Collins in 2008. After years of consistent efforts in the community and building relationships with key stakeholders, Collins announced in 2021 that the BMA would find a physical home in a bespoke music museum planned for Digbeth. Local cultural organisation Capsule have led another key project, Home of Metal, which culminated in exhibitions at the Birmingham Museum & Art Gallery (BMAG) and other venues in the Midlands in 2011 and 2019. Local organisations like the Westside Business Improvement District have also played a role in strengthening the city's music heritage through, for example, the Birmingham Walk of Stars and the Black Sabbath Bridge and Bench. A policy review by Birmingham City Council (2012, p. 13) discussed the potential that popular music might have in 'improving perceptions of Birmingham' for both visitors and residents. However, at the time of our fieldwork in 2019, participant responses suggested that the policy review did not result in any additional funding or support for music heritage projects.

1.3.3 Wollongong

Wollongong is situated on the east coast of Australia in the state of New South Wales. Located an hour's drive south of Sydney, Australia's most populous city, the Wollongong region is home to upwards of 260,000 people (Australian Bureau of Statistics, 2017). While Wollongong does not have the international reputation of Detroit and Birmingham, it offers an interesting comparative example as a deindustrialising city. From the late nineteenth to early twentieth centuries, the region's economy was based on dairy farming, coal mining and steel manufacturing (Hagan & Lee, 2002). The city's steelworks was its biggest employer from World War II until the 1970s, with migrant workers from the Middle East, Britain and Europe supporting the industry's growth (Barnes et al., 2006; Schultz, 1985; Waitt & Gibson, 2009; Watson, 1991). Due to global economic restructuring, from 1982 to 1983, there was a reduction of more than 20,000 jobs in Wollongong's steel and coal industries (Watson, 1991). By 1996, the size of the workforce at the steelworks was about a quarter of what it was in the 1970s (Hagan, 2002). As Hagan (2002, p. 165) observes, 'The end of the steel boom had severe effects on the Region, and the transition from forty years of boom to prolonged recession was painful.' As with our other case study cities, these economic struggles were exacerbated by the 2008–9 Global Financial Crisis, which Gibson (2013, p. 68) notes 'froze the global demand for steel' and yielded 'thousands of job losses' for Wollongong. Similar to Detroit and Birmingham, the impacts of deindustrialisation have been uneven across Wollongong, with Port Kembla – the suburb in which the steelworks is

Figure 1 Wentworth Street (Port Kembla's main street) looking towards the steelworks. Photo by Sarah Baker

located (see Figure 1) – exhibiting higher rates of social and economic disadvantage (Barnes et al., 2006).

In response to the declining steel industry, Wollongong's local government has led several efforts aimed at economic revival and urban reimagining. Wollongong rebranded itself as the 'Leisure Coast' in the 1980s and the 'City of Diversity' and 'City of Innovation' in the late 1990s (Barnes et al., 2006). In 2010, the city launched the 'We Love the Gong' marketing campaign in response to residents' negative perceptions of the area following a significant corruption scandal in the city council (Kerr et al., 2012). Wollongong is recognised as one of the first city councils in Australia to adopt a creative cities agenda for urban revitalisation, following other cities around the globe that were prioritising investment in cultural industries (Barnes et al., 2006; Waitt & Gibson, 2009; see also Florida, 2002). These strategies, in Wollongong and elsewhere, have often focused too heavily on 'attracting outside investment and appealing to new [creative class] residents' (Cantillon et al., 2021b, p. 105), which can marginalise existing residents (Barnes et al., 2006) and fail to acknowledge the '[f]ringe groups, amateurs, [and] community non-profit collectives' (Gibson et al., 2012, p. 288) that also constitute a city's creative milieu. Although Waitt and Gibson (2009) contend that creative city strategies have not been wholly successful in Wollongong, the city has nevertheless managed to diversify its economic base. Wollongong's key sectors of employment include

health, aged care, higher education, retail and iron smelting and steel manufacturing (Australian Bureau of Statistics, 2017). In particular, the University of
Wollongong has become one of the city's biggest employers. Our interviewees
noted the city has shifted from a 'steel city' to a 'university town' (Julie,
9 October 2018), while the steelworks continues to employ several thousand
people in the region.

Wollongong has strong rock, grunge and punk music traditions. Although its
music scene has been less globally influential as compared to Detroit and
Birmingham, local surf rock band Hockey Dad has found international success
since the late 2010s. Other prominent bands include Tumbleweed – who
supported Nirvana during their 1992 Australian Tour – as well as Sunday
Painters, Proton Energy Pills and Zambian Goat Herders. Heritage initiatives
have centred on The Oxford Tavern, an important local venue, including *The
Occy: A Doco* (Burling, 2012), an amateur documentary film, and *Friday Night
at the Oxford* (Humphries, 2018), a collection of stories from a local journalist.
However, Wollongong's most prolific popular music heritage initiative has been
Steel City Sound, an online archive active from 2010 to 2015 (and no longer
available as of late 2019) and its associated exhibition at the WAG held from
November 2014 to March 2015.

1.4 Research Methods

This Element draws on qualitative data collected during a multi-year project
(2017–21) on popular music heritage and cultural justice in deindustrialising
cities. Initially funded by the authors' university as a small-scale pilot study
focused on Wollongong, an international comparative version of the project was
the subject of a funding application for the Australian Research Council (ARC).
Although this project was recommended for funding by the ARC and its expert
reviewers in 2017, it was vetoed by the federal education minister along with ten
other humanities projects. In the wake of this political interference – an ironic
injustice given the focus of the research – the authors' university funded the
project at a reduced budget and timeline over 2019–20. Fieldwork took place in
Wollongong from 8 to 13 October 2018, 15 to 20 June 2019 and 16 to
23 October 2019; in Birmingham from 30 March to 2 April 2019 and
28 August to 15 September 2019; and in Detroit from 3 to 14 April 2019. Semi-
structured interviews were conducted with a total of thirty-six participants
across the three sites. Data collection also involved photographs and observa-
tions in each city, including visiting heritage institutions and attending exhibitions. As we discuss in detail in Section 4, the final fieldwork trip to
Wollongong included a public event at WAG facilitated by the authors.

The panel-style event featured research participants from all three case study cities, along with other experts in popular music heritage practice.

The project's participants included key 'gatekeepers' who were primary points of contact in Birmingham and Detroit: Jez Collins (BMA) and Carleton Gholz (DSC). Both are active leaders in the popular music heritage space in their respective cities, both were international partner investigators on the vetoed ARC version of this project and both have academic backgrounds. Jez, formerly an academic at Birmingham City University who completed a Master's thesis on online popular music archives as public history-making, has been involved in numerous writing projects with the authors, while Carleton completed a PhD on Detroit's music history before turning his attention to heritage practice. In Wollongong, there was no single key gatekeeper from the outset as the most notable heritage initiative that emerged from the city (Steel City Sound) was no longer in operation. Other participants in our research included professional and DIY heritage practitioners, heritage volunteers, journalists, historians, documentary makers, local government councillors and employees, former venue owners, festival organisers, record store operators and record label founders.

The research also incorporated the arts-based method of zine-making. Zines are self-published booklets with a DIY aesthetic comprising text, images and other materials. Zine-making is a 'research method that communicates back to the community' (Cele, 2021, p. 137; see also Baker & Cantillon, 2022). In this project, the zines served as a source of data, a process for analysing data and an accessible community engagement output. The first zine, *Sounds of Our Town: The Wollongong Edition* (Baker et al., 2020b), featured the transcript of the public panel held at WAG, the transcript of a radio interview with the research team and two participants, and written content that emerged from a zine workshop. The second zine, *Sounds of Our Town: The Detroit Edition* (Baker et al., 2020a), contained the research team's reflections on the fieldwork undertaken in Detroit, a photo essay on racial injustice, and some analytical work applying a cultural justice lens to Detroit's popular music heritage initiatives. The final zine, *Sounds of Our Town: The Birmingham Edition* (Buttigieg et al., 2020), included a Q&A with the founder of the BMA as well as a scholarly reflection and a poem from two Birmingham-based music heritage researchers. Content from the zines appears throughout the following sections. The public event and corresponding zines were an attempt to enact cultural justice as method (see Section 4).

Once the data was collected, the research team analysed the dataset using NVivo software. This process involved undertaking a thematic analysis to identify commonalities, differences and patterns relating to our preliminary framework for cultural justice: practices of collection and preservation, story-telling the past and the mobilising of communities. We focused on 'attending to the intricacies of the individual case', noting the 'diversity and variety' of cases, and questioning 'the reasons for variation or indeed for similarity across cases' (Filippucci, 2009, p. 322). In the sections that follow, we draw on a variety of popular music heritage activities in Birmingham, Detroit and Wollongong to highlight the extent to which the tools of cultural justice have materialised in these initiatives.

With backgrounds in sociology and cultural studies, our approach to project design, data collection and analysis has been informed by ongoing consideration of the implications of positionality in knowledge production (Rose, 1997). As such, we recognise the importance of providing a positionality statement that orients the reader to how we may have approached this research. The first and second authors are both white, second-generation Australian, middle-class, straight, cisgender women, and the third author is a white, third-generation French, working-class, straight, cisgender man. The first author grew up in the working-class industrial hub of Elizabeth, South Australia; the closure of the area's General Motors-Holden car manufacturing facility and component industries in 2017 was one of the events that inspired this research project (see Section 4). These dimensions of our individual and collective identities may have impacted the outcomes of our research in various ways. For example, our dominant racial and sexual identities could reduce our attentiveness to aspects of race or sexuality that we have not experienced directly, 'or that benefit us to others' detriment or exclusion' (Cantillon et al., 2017, p. 42). Given the project's focus on cultural justice, we sought to include interviewees from diverse backgrounds, including people of colour and neurodivergent and gender-diverse participants; to represent examples in our writing that amplify the histories and voices of marginalised groups; and to reflect critically on how we, our participants and various heritage initiatives may be perpetuating cultural injustices. Such an approach – orienting our methodology towards cultural justice – is reflected in the empirical and conceptual discussion of cultural justice in Sections 2 to 5, which unpack the complexities of how cultural justice is approximated, unfolds and falters.

1.5 Outline of the Structure of the Element

The following sections present the three overarching tools heritage practitioners might consider for pursuing cultural justice when undertaking popular music heritage initiatives in deindustrialising cities. The tools have been separated to aid in structuring the Element, with Sections 2, 3 and 4 exploring each tool's specificity. While in each section we draw on heritage initiatives to illustrate aspects of the tools, these initiatives are not provided as exemplars of the tools in action. Rather, the initiatives are analysed through the critical lens offered by the tool to tease out the relationship to cultural justice. We also recognise that the tools do, in fact, often overlap and intertwine in practice. Section 2 focuses on collection, preservation and archiving, with specific reference to the BMA, Steel City Sound and the DSC's activities to protect United Sound Systems Recording Studio and Blue Bird Inn. Section 3 turns to the storying of the past through an exploration of Home of Metal's 'Black Sabbath – 50 Years' temporary exhibition at BMAG, the Exhibit 3000 museum in Detroit, in situ markers such as the Birmingham Walk of Stars and Black Sabbath Bridge and Bench and bus tours run by the DSC and the BMA. Section 4 considers how communities of interest mobilise for collective action, taking a closer look at the collaborative, do-it-together approaches of the DSC, BMA and WAG, as well as our own efforts to enact cultural justice through a public event. The Element ends with a concluding section that sets out the cultural justice toolkit to guide future popular music heritage initiatives and scholarship.

2 Collection, Preservation and Archiving

Popular music heritage tends to emphasise material culture, with collections often focused on objects and ephemera that represent the style, aesthetics and memories associated with artists, bands, music scenes and local cultures (Leonard, 2007). Likewise, the intangible qualities of popular music heritage also come to be linked with tangible spaces such as music venues, recording studios and childhood homes or hangouts of artists. In this section, we focus on both the practices of collecting and archiving physical and digital artefacts of popular music cultures and the preservation of built heritage connected to popular music's past.

2.1 Archiving for Cultural Justice

Birmingham, Detroit and Wollongong have all been home to grassroots efforts to collect and document rich histories of popular music. Conceptualised as community archives, 'community participation, control and ownership' of these projects 'is essential' (Flinn, 2007, p. 153). Flinn and Stevens (2009, p. 6) assert that community archives are predominantly motivated by a belief that mainstream heritage organisations have failed to collect, make accessible and accurately reflect 'the stories of all of society'. They are the result of people yearning for 'the minor narratives, the untold stories, the traces, the whispers and the expressions of marginalized identities' that had not been adequately

captured in existing collections (Bastian & Alexander, 2009, p. xxiii). In
seeking to redress this imbalance, community archives are 'often viewed
explicitly as counter-hegemonic tools for education and weapons in the struggle
against discrimination and injustice' (Flinn & Stevens, 2009, pp. 6–7). The
records they hold can 'become the memory glue that binds people seeking to
recall and share similar experiences' (Bastian & Alexander, 2009, p. xxii).
A capacity for cultural justice therefore resides in a community archive's 'acts
of recovery' that 'rescue personal and social, collective histories from deliberate
and physical erasure' in ways that generate 'feelings of connectedness, ownership and community' within, and also beyond, the archive's communities of
interest (Flinn & Stevens, 2009, pp. 16, 17). The BMA and Steel City Sound
offer examples of community archives of popular music's past in our case study
cities.

2.1.1 Documenting Birmingham's Popular Music Past

The BMA is a non-profit heritage organisation originally started as an online
archive with the support of funding from an Arts Council England grant in
2008. Over the years, this self-authorised initiative has capitalised on one-off
grants from authorised heritage bodies and local government to expand the
BMA's activities to also include exhibitions, documentary films and other
heritage projects aligned with the online archive's core focus. The BMA's
online archive has sought to 'portray the scope of the city's popular music
heritage' (Collins, 2015, p. 82) through crowdsourced materials. With an aim
to appeal to 'anyone who identifies with the city of Birmingham' (Collins,
2015, p. 82), the BMA draws users in with the catchphrase 'Tell us what you
know, tell us what you think!' (Birmingham Music Archive, n.d.). The online
archive is supplemented by social media accounts on Facebook and Twitter,
which together have over 10,000 contributors generating thousands of entries,
posts and comments, including uploading their own digitised artefacts
(Collins, 2020a). Content is organised into categories including bands/musi-
cians, exhibitions, festivals, DJs/club nights/promoters, record labels, venues
and press/fanzines. Individual entries typically feature brief descriptive text,
a selection of images (photographs, posters) and comments contributed by the
site's users.

Jez, the archive's founder, describes his work with the BMA as a 'bottom-up
approach to history or archiving' in which 'there's nothing that's not deemed
important enough. I'm not interested, really, about right and wrong, I'm interested [in] "is there a space for you to tell us the things you did, and then we all
learn from it"' (Jez, cited in Baker et al., 2020b, p. 15). The aim is about more

than education, with Jez also emphasising the importance of the archive's approach for enhancing people's positive feelings about the city through content that is relatable and deeply personal. Speaking of gig flyers, Jez highlights that the artefacts of popular music's past are 'really important historical facts, and they play a role within civic pride ... people can look back and say, "Actually, you know I can see myself reflected in those materials"' (cited in Baker et al., 2020b, p. 9). In addition, the archive's approach is underscored by a commitment to accessibility. As one interviewee noted, 'you can be anywhere in the world and contribute your memories and anecdotes and memorabilia' to the BMA (Lyle, 12 September 2019), meaning it can have global input, reach and resonance as well as personal and localised affects.

For Jez, the critical questions for the collection and preservation of Birmingham's popular music past are 'Whose history? Who's telling it?' (cited in Baker et al., 2020b, p. 46). He emphasises that the BMA seeks to document and preserve Birmingham's music culture because 'it's all our histor-ies' (Jez, cited in Baker et al., 2020b, p. 45). This is not to say there is not also personal motivation underpinning at least the early activities of the BMA, with Jez reflecting that: 'I wanted to document bands like Nigel The Spoon who were my mates and played to about 30 people in a venue called The Barrel Organ. It was important to me to record bands and venues like these as they were *my* bands, *my* venues and helped form *my* cultural identity' (Collins, 2020b, p. 50, original emphasis). But the main thrust of the BMA is that 'history resides out there, in the people in the audience, and ... out there in the community' (Jez, cited in Baker et al., 2020b, p. 24). Maximising opportunities for communi-ties of interest to actively participate in the collection and preservation of the city's rich musical past is a key concern for Jez in the ongoing quest for cultural justice. Jez stresses that he 'need[s] to give some thought about how I really do increase the capacity of the BMA', particularly in relation to human resources – 'so they can do the scanning, so they can do the inter-views, so they can upload and put stuff on the site. That's a great need' (Jez, 1 April 2019). He also recognises that 'much more needs to be done' to make the archive a 'properly representative history of the real plurality of voices belonging to Birmingham and its communities', noting that the collection has 'large gaps in the Black and POC histories, as well as those of LGBT+ communities' which the BMA will 'need to address' for cultural justice to be experienced by those communities (Collins, 2020a, p. 21). There is, there-fore, both a desire and a need for increased participation to ensure the BMA is sustainable long term and to make the archive's content more inclusive and representative.

2.1.2 Archiving Wollongong's Music Scenes

A couple of years after Jez began his efforts to document Birmingham's popular music heritage, a similar initiative got underway in Wollongong by music enthusiast and community worker Warren Wheeler. Warren launched Steel City Sound in 2010 as an online archive that sought to capture the rich history of Wollongong's popular music past by way of blog posts that centred on notable local bands, venues, events and publications. Visitors to the site could learn about everything from bands like Babymachine to Zambian Goat Herders to venues such as Cabbage Tree Hotel and Zondrae's. Reflecting on the connections between music heritage and local identity, Warren wrote that the archive was underpinned by an understanding that:

> Documenting and archiving the sound of our city provides more than just a novel nostalgic trip for those that have since 'grown up' and moved on. It paints the story of Wollongong and our surrounds. It celebrates the creative spirit that the region cultivates and aims to ensure that the product of that spirit is preserved for future generations. (Wheeler, 2013a)

For Warren, the value of Steel City Sound was in its capacity to generate and affirm a sense of local identity beyond the city's boom and bust of steel manufacturing.

Warren describes Steel City Sound as his 'first attempt to archive' (12 October 2018). The idea for an online archive emerged from talking to an older friend about bands they had seen in Wollongong in the past: 'I just started saying "this stuff needs to be documented somewhere, someone needs to do something with this stuff" and she just said, "Why don't you do that?"' (Warren, 12 October 2018). Warren identified a gap in collecting practices and took it upon himself to create Steel City Sound in an effort to save these local music histories from being forgotten. He then set about the task of collecting material for the archive: 'I'd interview bands, I'd hunt down recordings, all sorts of interesting Wollongong-based stuff' (Warren, 12 October 2018). Initially only documenting music from his own past, the archive grew to include histories from the wider region (known as the Illawarra), posts informed by suggestions that visitors emailed to Warren, and posts from guest contributors.

Across the site, comments on posts featured not only people sharing their memories but also critiques of the archive. Most commonly, criticisms focused on missing bands. These concerns were echoed by some interviewees – for example, Scotty (18 June 2019) remarked that Steel City Sound 'doesn't tell the whole story. It doesn't catalogue all the bands'. In response to critical comments on the website, Warren reiterated that the archive's list of bands was not meant to be exhaustive. It is near impossible for any archive to be entirely comprehensive – a pursuit especially challenging for a DIY, self-authorised initiative. Community archives such as Steel City Sound are, more often than not, characterised by a lack of resources – 'financial, human, physical, skills, and expertise' (Flinn, 2011, p. 13) – which impact the capacity to fully document the subject at hand as well as the sustainability of the archival endeavour (as also noted in Section 2.1.1 in reference to the BMA).

Warren recognised that more help was needed to improve and maintain the archive. He sought funding from the local council, but these applications were unsuccessful. Subsequently, updates to the Steel City Sound website slowed from 2012. In a post from March 2013, Warren explained his absence:

> As it's been over seven months since any action took place here, I figured it only fair to provide everyone with an update. Truth is, 2012 was a difficult year for me personally. As was 2011 for that matter. Couple this with some uneccesarily [sic] political and, quite frankly, divisive actions by a select few people within the scene, the task of maintaining Steel City Sound became paralysing and the project unfortunately slipped into an unplanned hiatus. . . . During the unexpected time off I discovered that I am surrounded by an amazingly creative and supportive bunch of people. I now know that, whilst I may be the founder of this project, I am not in it alone. The negative comments and destructive behaviour of the minority do not reflect the broader publics [sic] appreciation of Steel City Sound. And as such I am ready to move forward. I have some big ideas for the project over the next little while, and hopefully you'll start to see some changes soon. (Wheeler, 2013a)

Here, Warren cites some of the difficulties he faced – personal issues, internal politics of music scenes – but also points to broader support and opportunities for collaboration (which eventually culminated in a Steel City Sound temporary exhibition at the WAG from 2014 to 2015, see Section 4).

By 2015, updates to the archive had ceased altogether. At the time of our interview with Warren in late 2018, the archive was dormant but still accessible, and he spoke of how it might be preserved into the future:

> I think maintaining that information, keeping that information available is important. I've often thought about how I could create some kind of portal where other people can put up information and what have you, but that obviously takes a lot of effort, a lot of work, fact checking and all that kind of stuff, and I haven't got time for that, and because there's no money in it, so it's almost for the love of it. (Warren, 12 October 2018)

It is common for DIY heritage initiatives to encounter challenges relating to long-term viability, particularly when they depend on the ongoing unpaid labour and commitment of individual enthusiasts (Baker & Collins, 2015). Shifting to a more participatory endeavour, like that of the BMA, was a logistical and financial challenge that Warren could not overcome. From a cultural justice perspective, public access is paramount; if archives cannot be engaged with or used as a resource, their impact is severely limited. Unfortunately, in the case of Steel City Sound, by 2019 its web hosting was no longer being paid. While the full archive can now only be accessed via internet archives like Wayback Machine, the WordPress prototype of the archive from 2010 remains available (see Wheeler, 2010).

2.2 Preserving Built Heritage in Detroit

Continuing usage of venues and recording spaces associated with a city's popular music culture can enable a 'cultural patina' (Schofield & Wright, 2021, p. 1) to develop. Intact buildings allow 'a tangible connection to be made with the scene's significant landmarks' (Schofield & Wright, 2021, p. 1), but when these buildings are left to decay, removed from their original site or are under threat of demolition, cultural patina is eroded. In Detroit, Herstad (2019) observed that 150 blighted buildings are demolished each week, mostly in the interest of creating space for new developments, and with little regard for a site's past or the value of these structures for remembering local histories and feeling a sense of attachment to place. In this section, we consider projects undertaken by the DSC that have strived to conserve, revitalise and draw attention to two significant examples of built heritage connected to the city's popular music history: the United Sound Systems Recording Studios and the Blue Bird Inn.

Proclaimed to be 'Michigan's oldest and Detroit's first independent recording studio' (Detroit Sound Conservancy, 2020c), United Sound Systems was the site of recordings for a wide range of notable artists, including Aretha Franklin, Miles Davis, Charlie Parker, John Lee Hooker, Parliament and the Red Hot Chili Peppers. Despite the studio 'go[ing] back to 1939', since 2013, a proposed freeway expansion has put the site at risk (Carleton, cited in Baker et al., 2020b, p. 8). In an effort to save United Sound Systems, the DSC and its community partners successfully lobbied for the site to become a local historic district in 2015. In 2017, the DSC led fundraising efforts to support the instalment of a Michigan Historic Marker, which indicates, in situ, the site's cultural and historical significance (see Figure 2). In this example, the DSC are pushing back against the pro-development, urban renewal agenda that has been so pervasive – and, at times, problematic – in Detroit's past and present pursuit of revitalisation (see also Herstad, 2017; Ryzewski, 2017). Herstad (2017, p. 96) notes that Detroit's local government has historically been underpinned by 'a culture of

Figure 2 United Sound Systems Recording Studios building and accompanying Michigan Historic Marker. Photo by Zelmarie Cantillon

clearance and the belief in demolition as progress' and still 'lacks a strong historic preservation program'. The city's blight removal and reclamation projects are often framed as a 'universal good' (Herstad, 2017, p. 86), but such initiatives can displace Black residents; 'eras[e] the material legacies of racism, segregation, and deindustrialization from the city's landscape' (p. 89); and fail to address the very structural economic and racial inequalities that contributed to urban decline in the first place. Fighting for the protection of built heritage in this context, then, represents an act of cultural justice. The Michigan Department of Transportation announced in 2019 that they had purchased the site in order to relocate it to an adjacent parking lot during the freeway expansion and, once those works are completed, the building is to be auctioned (Cwiek, 2019). While movement towards cultural justice is reflected in the commitment to preserve the United Sound Systems building, cultural injustice remains in the building's removal from the original site and its unknown future at auction. This is a reminder that cultural justice is an ongoing process which is pursued but not necessarily fully attained.

Another major built heritage project undertaken by the DSC has been the preservation of the Blue Bird Inn, purchased by the organisation in 2019. The building is located on Tireman Avenue (see Figure 3), a thoroughfare that 'served as the unofficial "Jim Crow Line" whereby African Americans' to the south 'were prevented from moving north', where the white community resided,

Figure 3 Blue Bird Inn, Detroit. Photo by Zelmarie Cantillon

'via racial covenants banning black home ownership' (City of Detroit, 2019, p. 2; see also Gonda, 2015). From the late 1930s through to the 1970s, the Blue Bird Inn hosted live music, being an important space for Black musicians to practice and perform. Throughout the 1940s and into the 1960s, it was a thriving jazz club, famous for hosting renowned performers including Charlie Parker, Miles Davis, Dorothy Ashby, Art Blakey, Betty Carter, John Coltrane, Alice Coltrane and Sarah Vaughn (Clark, 2020; National Park Service, 2019). At the peak of its activity in the 1940s, the Blue Bird Inn was 'a black-owned, working-class bar in the heart of the West Side black community' frequented by local residents, particularly factory workers (Macías, 2010, p. 49; see also Ryzewski, 2021). The preservation of buildings like the Blue Bird was on the agenda of the DSC since the organisation's conception: 'we knew … that if the DSC was going to matter we would have to eventually address buildings and histories like the Blue Bird's' (Detroit Sound Conservancy, 2020a). Carleton Gholz, founder of the DSC, observed that the restoration of the Blue Bird Inn 'is definitely not a nostalgic project' for the organisation, but one motivated by the question of 'how do we leverage things that we still remember, that are in our hearts, to keep our neighbourhoods?' (cited in Baker et al., 2020b, p. 12).

The building sat abandoned and in a state of disrepair for many years. It was added to the city's list of dangerous buildings in 2017 and subsequently slated for demolition (Detroit Sound Conservancy, 2021a). The purchase of the Blue Bird Inn for US$8,500 (Jordan, 2021) was made possible by a community development grant the DSC received from The Kresge Foundation. During fieldwork in Detroit in 2019, Carleton explained that there was a plan for the DSC to restore the building and use the space as a music archive and live music venue. One participant remarked that it was astonishing the building was still in a preservable state, observing that many of Detroit's 'wonderful heritage sites', including 'the Blue Bird, are open to the weather, and that's probably the biggest problem. You abandon a building and it goes bad real fast' (Joel, 5 April 2019). A key first task for the DSC was the urgent replacement of the building's roof, which was completed in 2021 following a fundraising campaign. Due to continued efforts by the DSC, in 2020 the Blue Bird Inn was designated a local historic district in recognition of its significance in relation to National Register of Historic Places criteria around its associations with historic events, notable people from the past and capacity to yield important information about local African American history (see City of Detroit, 2019). In 2022, the DSC was awarded three additional significant grants to realise its vision of rehabilitating and reopening the Blue Bird 'as a neighborhood hearth for the community in the form of a music venue, gathering space and cultural education center' (Detroit Sound Conservancy, 2022): $150,000 in implementation funding from The Kresge Foundation, $100,000 from the African American Cultural Heritage Action Fund and $30,000 from the Detroit Regional Chamber and General Motors' NeighborHUB grants.

Prior to purchasing the building, the DSC, with funding from Detroit Creative Corridor, had dedicated significant effort to preserving another piece of the Blue Bird Inn – the venue's iconic stage. Preservation of the stage is particularly important given the Blue Bird Inn's 'historic interior has been completely scrapped, leaving few vestiges of the historic nightclub' that can act as tangible reminders of the musical activity that once took place there (City of Detroit, 2019, p. 8). After restoring the stage, the DSC made it available as a 'modular, mobile, programming and exhibit experience' to be curated and toured (Detroit Sound Conservancy, 2020a). Talking about the refurbishment of the stage, Joel (5 April 2019) commented on its power to spark an affective response: 'I get to that stage and I'm kind of – the number of people that walked across that stage, as a jazz fan, I'm just – you know, "incredible"'. The Blue Bird's stage holds enormous material and symbolic significance as 'an exceptional example of African American mid-century vernacular art and design as well as a launchpad for sonic and social rebellion during the Civil Rights movement in Detroit' (Detroit Sound Conservancy, 2020a). The DSC plans to return the stage to its original home once the Blue Bird Inn refurbishment is completed.

Saving and restoring the Blue Bird Inn illustrates the DSC's quest for cultural justice in that it recognises and respects the venue's significant musical legacy while also striving to ensure that this space can be a source of local pride in the present and into the future. The case of the Blue Bird Inn also highlights how music heritage can be deeply connected to – and, therefore, leveraged to address – broader issues of justice relating to systemic racism, class inequalities and industrial decline. With the local government not viewing this area of Detroit as a 'strategic neighbourhood', what was once called the Old West Side or the Black West Side 'literally ... doesn't have a name anymore' (Carleton, cited in Baker et al., 2020b, p. 22). For Carleton, the restored building will serve as 'an inconvenient reminder of a hundred-year history [of the Black West Side] that hopefully can't be removed anytime soon' (cited in Baker et al., 2020b, p. 22). In this way, the 'uncomfortable history' of popular music, as represented by the Blue Bird Inn as a significant historical venue, can be used as a way to 'push back' against the idea that neighbourhoods like the Old West Side are 'blank slates' (Carleton, cited in Baker et al., 2020b, p. 22).

When asked about neighbourhood perceptions of the work the DSC was doing with the Blue Bird Inn, Carleton (12 April 2019) was 'cautiously optimistic that people think it's very exciting that the building is coming back'. For example, a collaboration between the DSC and a local neighbourhood group, the Larchmont Community Association, has provided residents with an opportunity to contribute ideas for the venue's future, with resident feedback indicating a need for the Blue Bird to become a community centre in addition to a place for live music and archival holdings (Clark, 2020). Carleton is highly reflexive about the challenges of this kind of cultural justice work and recognised that, initially, community responses to the DSC's presence were also shaped by him being a white heritage activist – as the founder and often the 'face' of the organisation – undertaking preservation projects in a historically Black community (see Section 4, however, for a discussion of the DSC's diverse board of directors). He also described how – understandably, given the history of the Old West Side – the older generation may be jaded and cynical about restoration efforts, taking a 'seeing is believing' view of the project: 'they are, sort of, "Yeah, call me when it's open"' (Carleton, 12 April 2019). Carleton noted that when people see the restored stage, the mission of the DSC becomes very clear in terms of what it means to preserve the legacy of this venue: 'they're hooked. The problem is, we haven't had enough opportunity to engage residents' (12 April 2019). Even with projects that are directly shaped by a commitment to cultural justice, getting 'buy-in' from communities can take time. Carleton is very aware that there will be people in the neighbourhood who are cautious or critical, saying

It's inevitable because ... people feel so forgotten. And [the DSC is] not meeting basic needs, at the end of the day. We're not bringing 55 jobs or 100 jobs. Not even ten jobs. We can't solve crime. We can't solve historical hurt. (12 April 2019)

Members of this community, and those in neighbouring Black communities, are 'struggling to keep their water from being shut off, they're struggling to keep their water clean, they're struggling to stay in their homes' due to foreclosures (Carleton, cited in Baker et al., 2020b, p. 12). The complex history and contemporary lived experience of the Old West Side, filled with past and present injustices, means that heritage projects invite 'a very complicated dialogue' (Carleton, 12 April 2019). As Carleton explained, even locals who are happy to see that the Blue Bird Inn now has a future beyond dereliction may feel sad or conflicted because the thrust for preservation did not come from within the neighbourhood itself.

2.3 Conclusion

The archival work of the BMA and Steel City Sound and the building conservation initiatives of the DSC highlight how these efforts to collect and preserve are underpinned by a desire to democratise heritage practices. These examples seek to challenge cultural domination at all stages of heritage work – planning, community engagement, crowdsourcing materials, delivery and so on – through an emphasis on participatory practice and saving histories that have been overlooked and undervalued. It is also clear that in each case, cultural justice is a fluid *process* rather than a singular event or static achievement. The act of archiving the materials of popular music's past or preserving its built heritage contribute to the process of bringing greater cultural justice to/for communities of interest through, for example, enhancing recognition of and respect for particular histories that have been at risk of being lost, forgotten, demolished. While cultural justice principles evidently underpin the work of Jez, Warren and Carleton, each recognised the very real challenges of 'achieving' cultural justice outcomes more broadly for their communities of interest. As Carleton remarked, 'It's not just like, "Yay! Heritage! This solves all this," you know?' (12 April 2019). Efforts to collect and preserve the tangible and intangible records of popular music's past may not be enough to counter deeply entrenched injustices – the 'historical hurt' referred to by Carleton (12 April 2019) – and, in the case of building restoration, the unintended consequences of development activity must be considered. As a member of the Larchmont Community Association said in relation to the DSC's efforts with the Blue Bird Inn, 'We want development without displacement. We don't want the gentrifying piece' (cited in Clark, 2020). However, what these efforts of archiving and building restoration achieve is an opening up of possibilities for cultural justice in terms of providing opportunities for remembrance and memorialisation, community participation, learning through engagement with these resources and places and the return of a community's cultural patina.

3 Curation, Storytelling and Heritage Interpretation

Storytelling gives context to the tangible and intangible forms that popular music heritage takes. Stories can be communicated in a multitude of formats, including exhibitions, books, documentaries, tours and in situ interpretive tools such as plaques and signs. Practices of popular music heritage curation can produce narratives that encompass a variety of voices and experiences. From a cultural justice perspective, it is critical to question whose voices and experiences are being foregrounded and whose are downplayed or left out, as well as how and why these stories are being told. Storytelling can, for instance, rest on a limited number of 'official' voices that serve to reproduce well-established social and cultural hierarchies (Gentry & Smith, 2019). In this section, we explore how the storying of popular music's past has been deployed in deindustrialising cities in ways that reassert or make visible aspects of history that have been neglected or forgotten. We first consider examples of popular music exhibitions in Birmingham and Detroit, before turning to in situ interpretive tools and tours in these two cities.

3.1 Exhibiting Popular Music's Past in Birmingham and Detroit

In *Curating Pop*, Baker and colleagues (2019) present eight components involved in the curation of popular music heritage in museums: celebrating dominant and hidden histories; economies and the museum experience; influence of place; display of material culture; narratives of exhibitions; curator subjectivity; use of nostalgia; and inclusion of sound. Each of these components can serve a pursuit of cultural justice, but equally Baker and colleagues (2019) highlight how, in structuring popular music exhibitions, these components can also reinforce cultural injustices for communities of interest. For example, desires to celebrate lesser known artists or scenes and present the hidden histories of popular music are often overridden by an institutional need to attract visitors by recounting more familiar stories that reinforce a canon of star performers, mainstream genres, well-known venues and time periods or geographical locations that have already been determined to be central to the music industry. Canonic representations, often an outcome of economic rationalisations, impact understandings of racialised, classed and gendered contributions to popular music's past. Baker and colleagues (2019, p. 158) conclude that there is still much work to do in the curation of popular music exhibitions in terms of 'generating more nuanced and inclusive versions of history' in ways that 'recognize the malleability of popular music's meaning, roles and uses over time'. Next, we discuss two examples of popular music heritage exhibitions – Home of Metal's 'Black Sabbath – 50 Years' Exhibition in Birmingham and Exhibit 3000 in Detroit – which amplify issues of class and race through their narratives.

3.1.1 Home of Metal's 'Black Sabbath – 50 Years' Exhibition

Home of Metal's 'Black Sabbath – 50 Years' was held from June to September 2019 at BMAG. The exhibition was developed by the Birmingham-based arts organisation Capsule, perhaps best known for hosting Supersonic, a long-running experimental music festival. Capsule (2020), which describes itself as having a 'DIY ethos', had previously curated the exhibition 'Home of Metal – 40 Years of Heavy Metal' at BMAG from June to September 2011. 'Black Sabbath – 50 Years' is the second instalment in the Home of Metal heritage project, which, as was the case with the 2011 exhibition, also incorporated numerous other exhibitions and events held 'off venue' across Birmingham and the West Midlands. For example, the Midlands Arts Centre hosted 'Hands of Doom', which showcased portraits of Black Sabbath fans wearing hand-decorated 'battle jackets'; the New Art Gallery Walsall hosted an exhibition that incorporated recreated bedrooms of heavy metal fans; and the Parkside Gallery displayed portraits of metal fans from across the world.

The main Home of Metal exhibition, 'Black Sabbath – 50 Years', focuses on the origins, influence and legacy of Black Sabbath, crediting them for creating 'a new sound, a new aesthetic, and a new musical culture – Heavy Metal' (Capsule, 2019b). The exhibition begins its story by establishing the social, political, economic and urban context from which Black Sabbath emerged. Just beyond the exhibition's entrypoint (an enormous glittery gold Black Sabbath sign intended as a background for a 'Sabbath Selfie'), one of its first segments was devoted to the band's 'humble beginnings' (Capsule, 2019b) in 1960s Aston, Birmingham. This room drew attention to the working-class origins of Black Sabbath's band members, with a series of photographs depicting Aston's bombsites, factories and housing. A projection on the wall captured what it was like to work in the region's factories at this time. One volunteer described how the exhibition represented the experience of living in Birmingham in the late 1960s and early 1970s, 'where there were factories and plumes of smoke and

just how awful it was to live there at that time and just that kind of dirty feeling'
and the impact of industry 'on the culture of those artists that were ... in that
environment' (Adam, 7 September 2019). Another volunteer explained how
this room highlights the extent to which the soundscape of manufacturing
industries shaped metal music:

> [I]n that one room, where it shows you in the late 1960s, and that rumbling
> noise of the factories that everybody heard through the years ... it's to show
> them that that's what it came from. ... It's like industrial metal. Industrial
> metal came definitely from that, because that's what it is – it's sounds of
> industry: horrible, breaking, crushing of things. (Mark, 2 September 2019)

Text on another wall of this room retold the infamous story of how guitarist
Tony Iommi severed two of his fingertips in an accident while working in one of
the city's factories. As the text described: 'Tony created his own crude false
fingertips from melted plastic washing up liquid caps, covered in leather. In
time, Tony would down tune his guitar, loosening the string so they were more
comfortable for him to play. The metal-bashing of heavy industry directly
shaped the sound of Heavy Metal' (Capsule, 2019c). One interviewee posed,
'if he wouldn't have had the accident, would you have metal [music] as it is?
Probably not' (Adam, 7 September 2019).

In this first room of the exhibition, the curators were establishing how
socio-economic conditions are implicated in cultural production and creative
expression. Subsequent segments of the exhibition connected the band's early
music-making to other influences both local and global, including not only
musical acts but also film and literature (specifically, the horror genre),
Satanism, dissonance with hippie counterculture ('The hippy message of
dropping out of mainstream society was one that often felt out of touch with
the reality of working people's lives' (Capsule, 2019a)), the Vietnam War and
the women's liberation and American civil rights movements. Beyond this,
the exhibition focused significantly on the histories, experiences, myths and
idiosyncrasies of Black Sabbath's core band members, with displays featuring
on-stage costumes, instruments, technical equipment and images and video of
the band performing. Another section focused on the band's harsh reviews
from mainstream music critics, who labelled Black Sabbath as 'basic', 'loud'
and 'brash' – as Lester Bangs put it, music from 'unskilled laborers' (Capsule,
2019d). These criticisms were counterposed by the more favourable perspectives of audiences; an exhibition wall featured a quote from Geezer Butler
stating: 'The more the press hated us, the more the fans loved us' (Capsule,
2019d). Fan culture and its legacies were the focus of the final portion of the
exhibition, which displayed Black Sabbath-inspired artwork, a 1989

newsletter by the Black Sabbath Fan Club, collectors' items (e.g. band tees, figurines and other merchandise) from individual fans, and a wall of photographs of fans from around the world taken by Home of Metal volunteers during Black Sabbath's final tour. The story being constructed was that Black Sabbath, and metal, disrupted mainstream values and elite cultural sensibilities. The emphasis on fan cultures throughout the BMAG exhibition (and its off-venue counterparts) further reinforced the theme that Black Sabbath was a band that resonated with working-class experiences.

For the exhibition's volunteers, telling Black Sabbath's origin story also connected to a broader narrative of Birmingham's cultural vitality and the grit of its people, both of which are referred to as having emerged from the conditions of the industrial city. As Richard (6 September 2019) put it, 'We're going back to the raw ingredients, I guess, that made what has become the biggest export of the area.' Such storytelling works to transform negative stereotypes of Birmingham – those from its industrial heyday as well as those that have emerged from the city's deindustrialisation – for community members who, by way of the exhibition, are given permission to 'celebrate that "I'm from Birmingham and this is the home of metal"' (Adam, 7 September 2019).

The exhibition's presence in BMAG, a heritage building from 1885 renowned for its collection of Pre-Raphaelite paintings, is striking in its disruption of a high art/popular culture binary. Referring to both the 2011 and 2019 Home of Metal exhibitions, one BMAG employee noted that the focus on heavy metal music 'attracts a very different audience to what we normally have in the museum' (Katie, 3 September 2019). A volunteer for the 2019 exhibition expressed that 'Black Sabbath – 50 Years' opened up this building to an audience who may not have traditionally frequented BMAG because heavy metal is 'the music of the people. It's working class' (Bill, 3 September 2019). Cultural justice is not enacted simply by the inclusion of a non-traditional subject in the authorised heritage institution; the particular presentation of that subject for the communities of interest is also important. The display of popular music's past in authorised heritage institutions is frequently informed by art museum practices (Leonard, 2007) which, while aiding the legitimation of popular music ephemera as heritage, can be exclusionary for non-traditional gallery or museum audiences. In 'Black Sabbath – 50 Years', however, rather than letting the material culture of Black Sabbath 'speak for themselves as autonomous aesthetic objects' (Leonard, 2007, p. 155), the curators produced an exhibition rich in contextualisation whereby artefacts were situated in a place-based and classed narrative. The exhibition was regarded as particularly important for the younger generation since the city's popular music past is 'not really part of our education', which Richard argued was because the cultures of working-class people are not valued (6 September 2019). For Adam, the exhibition 'reinvigorate[d] the sense of place' of Birmingham (7 September 2019).

However, our interviewees also reported lingering cultural injustices which they had observed themselves or had gauged from visitor responses. For example, concerns were raised about the limitations of what could be achieved by an exhibition that was not permanent (Bill, 3 September 2019). Other critiques were centred on the exhibition only focusing on one band (Richard, 6 September 2019), and only on the 'first eight years' of that band's fifty-year history (Adam, 7 September 2019; Brittany, 31 August 2019). Moreover, while the exhibition brought to the fore the classed experience of the city, it was said to have done so in a way that provided 'a very white reading of musical culture' (Jez, 6 September 2019). Jez drew attention to the narrative presented around Tony Iommi's factory accident and how factory noise came to be reflected in the creative outputs of Black Sabbath. While Jez agrees that this is the case, he also recognises that these narratives can present a homogenous view of the creativity of Birmingham's factory workers given Iommi 'was working on the same bench presses, in the same factories as Black, Indian, Pakistani people and they weren't making "heavy" music, they were creating ska, bluebeat and reggae or Bhangra and Qawwali music' (Collins, 2020b, p. 49). In drawing attention to a music culture originating from white male factory workers, whose cultural histories had limited exposure in Birmingham's authorised heritage spaces, the narrative created in 'Black Sabbath – 50 Years', and the earlier 2011 exhibition, obscured the existence of racialised experiences of factory workers and their music-making. For Jez, those histories remained hidden. Despite these issues, interviewees agreed that the exhibition's connection to BMAG served to legitimise the genre of heavy metal as culturally important for Birmingham and subsequently provided recognition of the contributions of working-class people to Birmingham's cultural fabric.

3.1.2 Exhibit 3000

Located in an unassuming, three-storey square brick building at 3000 E. Grand Boulevard is the mecca of techno music in Detroit (see Figure 4). The building is home to the Underground Resistance music collective – 'the Public Enemy of Techno' (John, 12 April 2019), with strong political themes – including their record labels Submerge and Somewhere in Detroit, along with Exhibit 3000, the 'world's first and only techno museum' (Exhibit 3000, 2020). Accessible by appointment only, one of the book's authors received a guided tour from DJ, producer and curator John Collins. The museum primarily occupies an open

Figure 4 Exterior of Detroit's Exhibit 3000. Photo by Zelmarie Cantillon

plan room lined with display cabinets of photographs, vinyls, CDs, brochures, ticket stubs, books, instruments (sequencers, keyboards) and other memorabilia, along with a lathe behind a glass window that was bequeathed to them by record cutter Ron Murphy. Gesturing to these items, John told stories about legendary figures such as Juan Atkins ('the godfather' of techno), Derrick May, Eddie Fowlkes and Kevin Saunderson. Stopping at the display of DJs and producers, John highlighted the contribution of Stacey Hale. He noted that while 'back in the day DJing was probably more men than women', Stacey Hale was:

> one of the first female DJs in Detroit who got any recognition in the club scene. She can play just as good as these guys and probably outplay most of them. She still plays to this day. A lot of women have gotten into DJing as a result of her. She's a role model for women and teaches classes, all kinds of stuff. So that's why she's in our museum. (12 April 2019)

Moving on to a display about Underground Resistance, John discussed the display's recognition of influences on the collective's sound, highlighting the likes of Kraftwerk and Public Enemy. John emphasised that these influences were connected to the music of Underground Resistance having a social and political conscience, with, for example, tracks created with First Nations people. This music was also described as radiating outwards beyond Detroit, particularly in regard to the fall of the Berlin Wall, with John stating that Underground Resistance's music helped 're-energise or re-start the art scene' in Berlin. Pointing to an image of Underground Resistance's tour of Germany in 1991, John said 'some people credit Berlin with techno, which is not true'. The display provides a correction to that origin narrative. The final stop on the tour was the basement – a record store featuring a collection of techno vinyls, turntables and messages from fans and visitors scrawled on the walls and ceiling: 'You changed the way I hear', 'Thanks for a soundtrack for my life', 'Long live Detroit techno'.

The founding of Exhibit 3000 was instigated by a past temporary exhibition at the Detroit Historical Museum, for which John acted as a consultant. Running from January 2003 to August 2004, 'Techno: Detroit's Gift to the World' showcased 'the twenty year history of techno' by way of 'the stories of the DJs, producers, and other key figures in the manufacturing and promotion of techno music' (Che, 2009, p. 272). John explained:

> [I]t was a really, really, really good exhibit and I think the plan was that it would stay in Detroit for maybe one or two years and then travel around the world – well, it never left Detroit. ... [Exhibit 3000] was Mike Banks' [co-founder of Underground Resistance] idea. He said, 'You know, I'm going to do a museum here. I'm going to make sure that the accurate stories are being told.' ... it's a good thing he had that foresight because that exhibit ended, and if we hadn't done the one here, there'd be no techno museum anywhere, because this is the only one in the world. (John, 12 April 2019)

Here, John stresses the significance of the DIY approach to heritage whereby enthusiasts take on the role of custodians of popular music's past, saving material from being thrown away and forgotten, and safeguarding objects, stories and memories for future generations (Baker, 2018). In this case, Exhibit 3000's origins were in authorised heritage practice, but a self-authorised activity was necessary to ensure ongoing access to and curation of Detroit's techno history. Although Mike had no special expertise in heritage, John noted that they received assistance from Mike's sister Bridgette, who 'went to university specifically for that', and from academic Carla Vecchiola, whose PhD focused on Detroit's electronic music scene and community pride (see Vecchiola, 2006). Speaking further about Bridgette, John noted that 'luckily [she] kept fliers, old magazines, newspaper articles about the different groups and DJs ... t-shirts and all kinds of stuff, which some people would probably just throw away'. Such ephemera and everyday objects of music culture can become significant over time, acting as powerful triggers for remembering and storytelling. In describing the origins of Exhibit 3000, John emphasised a team effort involving John, Bridgette, Mike, Carla and Cornelius

Harris (who also runs guided tours at the museum), in addition to other enthusiasts who donated or loaned objects. The do-it-together (Collins, 2015) aspect of the DIY approach provides a strong foundation for cultural justice, illustrating how vital democratisation, participation and collectivity are, not only to founding and running community-based heritage initiatives but also to constructing narratives that are produced by and represent multiple voices.

John emphasised a strong desire for the museum to be accessible (in terms of entry being affordable, e.g. optional donation only) and sustainable ('it's not going anywhere') (12 April 2019). Both of these are important for the museum's central mission: education. For John, telling the 'true story of techno ... as it relates to the city Detroit, what it means to Detroit, how it came from Detroit', must take into account the 'African American experience, the influencers' (12 April 2019). It is important to share and conserve these stories 'so that history won't be changed', so that the creativity of Black Detroiters is not written out of techno's origin story:

> [A] lot of people have no idea that techno's created by Black people. They naturally assume it was white people ... they're blown away when they find out that it was created by Black people and I think that when techno was created it was about the Black experience, it was afrofuturistic as well. (John, 12 April 2019)

As John explained it, Exhibit 3000's contribution to Detroit's heritage landscape goes beyond techno. In a country where 'people of colour' are frequently 'written out of history' and their 'contributions have been glossed over', Exhibit 3000 offers a space to push back against dominant whitewashed narratives – 'we've got to educate' (John, 12 April 2019).

In highlighting Black creativity, Exhibit 3000 – along with other techno-focused initiatives in the city, such as the Detroit Electronic Music Festival – offers a narrative that counters the more traditional framing of Detroit as dominated by 'racial and economic problems' (Che, 2008, p. 201). As Vecchiola (2011, p. 111) states, Exhibit 3000 recognises 'the lives of Detroiters that are exemplary Americans – entrepreneurs, innovators, good citizens, lively ambassadors, thoughtful neighbors, community activists'. In doing so, Exhibit 3000 'shows that innovative, technological, creative, and grassroots approaches to urban crisis are the unrecognized strengths' of an otherwise 'besieged' city (Vecchiola, 2011, pp. 106–7). As was the case with the temporary exhibition at Detroit Historical Museum that inspired the creation of Exhibit 3000, the aim of John and his colleagues is to 'inspire youth to believe that they too can be creative and successful, whether or not that creativity is expressed through music or other avenues' (Che, 2009, p. 273).

Through its focus on the past, Exhibit 3000 is underpinned by cultural justice in its reassertion of the significance of Detroit in the narrative of techno's history and development. By way of storytelling, it also plays an active role in striving for cultural justice in the present, elevating and educating about the Black experience and creativity – a pursuit that reverberates in contemporary social and political circumstances.

3.2 In Situ Interpretive Tools and Tours

Another form of storytelling is via in situ markers and tours which constitute interpretive processes that 'heritagise' the urban environment, signalling and reinforcing popular music's significance to local communities and urban identity. For example, in situ interpretation can be found in Legends Plaza outside the Detroit Historical Museum, where local musicians' handprints are moulded in cement (see Figure 5). In Birmingham, interviewees emphasised the usefulness of in situ interpretative tools such as blue plaques placed to commemorate a building's role as a venue or in an artist's life. Such markers serve to make popular music's past 'more visible' in the cityscape – they are 'literal place-makers to help place-making' (Jez, 1 April 2019). However, as Roberts and Cohen (2015, p. 228) observe, 'plaques are bound by practical, bureaucratic and organizational challenges and constraints related to material geographies or

Figure 5 Legends Plaza, Detroit. Photo by Zelmarie Cantillon

landscapes of heritage'. While the delivery of cultural justice outcomes in deindustrialising cities requires 'more than just a plaque' (Jez, 1 April 2019), these signifiers are, as another interviewee highlighted, 'better than nothing' (Bill, 3 September 2019).

Birmingham's Broad Street – a main thoroughfare and nightlife precinct in the city – offers several examples of in situ interpretive tools. Walking down Broad Street, one can find the Birmingham Walk of Stars underfoot. Plaques affixed in the pathway pay tribute to musicians including Noddy Holder of rock band Slade; members of Electric Light Orchestra; bhangra singer Malkit Singh; each member of Black Sabbath; and the singers Jamelia, Toyah Willcox, Beverley Knight and Joan Armatrading. Where Broad Street crosses the Old Main Line of the canal is the Black Sabbath Bridge and Black Sabbath Bench, which features the faces of Geezer, Ozzy, Tony and Bill positioned so visitors can take photos sitting next to the bandmates' likeness (see Figure 6). All three initiatives – the stars, the bench and the naming of the bridge – were spearheaded by a local organisation, the Westside Business Improvement District (WBID), to bolster tourism in the area. The location of these initiatives have no specific connection to the band's history; however, interviewees described the work of WBID as

Figure 6 Black Sabbath Bench and Bridge, Birmingham. Photo by Zelmarie Cantillon

a series of 'really good initiatives', with the showcasing of Black Sabbath working to bring greater focus to Birmingham's role in the country's cultural offer (Adam, 7 September 2019). For example, one interviewee emphasised the intergenerational affordance of the bench in terms of educating Birmigham's children about Black Sabbath:

> There were three little girls running around and the dad was sayíng, . . . 'Go and sit down on this.' 'Well, what for, dad?' 'It's Black Sabbath.' 'Who are Black Sabbath?' 'You've never heard of Black Sabbath? Black Sabbath are one of the biggest bands to come out of Birmingham.' 'Oh, is it?' 'Yes. You know Ozzy Osbourne?' She goes, 'Oh, off the telly?' 'Yeah, that's him there. Look.' . . . So they all went and sat with Ozzy. (Bill, 3 September 2019)

Whereas this interviewee saw the bench as giving life to the next generation of Black Sabbath fans, another lamented that bench dedications are usually symbols of death:

> If you go to any park or a place around England, if you see a bench, there's a little plaque on it saying, 'Dee-der-der-der-der lived between this and this and they enjoyed sitting here.' And a bench, for me, is when somebody's died – but metal is alive and well and it's living in each and every person that comes from this time, that comes from the Midlands. Metal music is not dead and, for me, that bench – as much as it was a good thing – is a bad thing because the bench is symbolic – for me, they're always dedicated to dead people. (Richard, 6 September 2019)

Richard's comment points to the complexity of cultural justice work. The bench at once elevates the presence of Black Sabbath in the city, but also symbolically suggests that the band members, heavy metal and its association to the city are somehow fixed or of the past.

The presence – or even absence – of visual place-makers like blue plaques can be made more visible during tours. In Detroit, Carleton ran a 'Sound Tour' to accompany the Salvaging Sound exhibition held at Detroit Historical Museum. Attendees were guided through key sites relating to the city's sonic history, such as United Sound Systems, Blue Bird Inn, Grande Ballroom and the Motown headquarters. Also highlighted on the tour were places that have since been destroyed, such as Club Heaven at 7 Mile and Woodward, where a fast-food restaurant now stands. Going past the site, Carleton explained that Club Heaven was a significant nightlife venue for queer people in Detroit from the mid-1980s to mid-1990s, as well as being connected to the emergence of house and techno music. The origins of this tour lie in the Detroit Music Tour, which Slager (2020) notes had its first pilot run in 2012 as a collaboration between Jocelyn Ninneman and the DSC for Detroit's Allied Media Conference.

These tours emphasise a cultural justice approach to narrating the built heritage of Detroit's popular music past. As Slager (2020, p. 134) observes:

> Ninneman and Gholz are very up front in their criticism of urban renewal policies and other political economic forces that produced the landscape visible in the city, and they discuss racism, dispossession, and gentrification directly. Including empty lots and shuttered theaters alongside extant recording studios and other still-operating sites as they do allows them to acknowledge the devastation wrought by urban renewal, particularly against communities of color, and to recognize the significance of sites that have not survived to Detroit's resilient and still-active music communities.

Similarly, the narration in the 2019 tour emphasised the social, economic and geographic context of Detroit music's past and present. As the bus made its way through different neighbourhoods – some struggling, laden with abandoned buildings and empty lots, others in a process of regeneration or gentrification – the tour's participants learned of the effects of property foreclosures on communities, how highway developments were ripping through neighbourhoods, and the impact restricted housing covenants had historically on the rhythms of the city. In these ways, the story of Detroit's music heritage as well as its capacity for contemporary music-making is explicitly linked to racialised and classed experiences of the city, the impacts of deindustrialisation, the push for urban revitalisation and the consequences of gentrification.

In Birmingham, Jez takes people on a minivan tour he describes as 'a musical journey of the imagination' in that 'the places we're going to, most of them don't exist anymore, because they've been knocked down, re-purposed, removed' (1 April 2019). The tour undertaken by one of the authors began at the former site of 'legendary' music venue Mothers, located in the suburb of Erdington, north-east of Birmingham's city centre (Jez, 1 April 2019). Although only open from 1968 to 1971, the club was 'voted the best rock club in the world by Billboard Magazine in America', hosting the likes of Led Zeppelin, Pink Floyd, Black Sabbath, The Who, Elton John, Free, Richie Havens and DJ John Peel (Jez, 1 April 2019). Jez pointed out that, despite this musical significance and the potential for it to cultivate a sense of 'cultural pride' in the area, the site is not much to look at today – a bedding clearance outlet located above a grocery store, with a blue plaque that is barely visible, having been painted over (see Figure 7). The tour continued to Aston, where Jez showed the exterior of Ozzy Osbourne's childhood home and school as well as a space where Black Sabbath used to rehearse in a church basement. Moving on from these predominantly white neighbourhoods and music histories, the tour headed north-west to Handsworth, where Jez explained how reggae music – and, specifically, Steel Pulse – were borne out of the more 'mixed' community of Black, Asian and

Figure 7 Traces of a blue plaque on the building that was formerly the location of Mothers, a Birmingham music venue. Photo by Zelmarie Cantillon

white people who 'work[ed] in those factories together', creating 'a multiplicity of sounds' in these areas (1 April 2019). One of the stops on the tour was Handsworth Park, where Punch Records has contributed to the recognition of the diversity of Birmingham's music culture and the neighbourhood's Black community through a mural commemorating Steel Pulse and the group's record Handsworth Revolution (see Figure 8).

Driving along Soho Road, Jez offered perhaps the most salient example of the heterogeneity of Birmingham's music cultures. Jez directed attention to bhangra, 'a form of Punjabi folk music ... overlaid with reggae lines and English guitar lines', which emerged from diverse communities living, working and socialising together in the area, creating new forms of cultural production and consumption (1 April 2019). Jez's incorporation of the histories of Steel Pulse, reggae and other genres which contained the sounds of reggae served to highlight cultural diversity and experiences of racism in Birmingham. While the tour included expected white artists like Black Sabbath, Jez observed that the city's contributions to British reggae are 'something that we've never, ever appreciated or celebrated, which to me is absolutely incredible because it is nationally, I think, one of the most important sounds' (1 April 2019).

Jez's minivan tour, like the Detroit Sound Tour, enabled less visible histories to be illuminated in a different way than in an archive or exhibition – drawing attention to the layers of history in situ, grounded in their urban context and

Figure 8 Steel Pulse mural in Handsworth Park. Photo by Zelmarie Cantillon

attendant sights, sounds, people, activities and rhythms. A commitment to tenets of cultural justice is evident in the stories being told on these tours. However, this method for storytelling comes with its own problems. As Jez explained, he is conscious that these sites of popular music heritage are located in places where people are going about their everyday lives and may not feel comfortable being subjected to the tourist gaze:

> [T]his is not a well off area. . . . I pull up in a big van and people are taking photos and . . . they don't know who you are. You could be from the government, police. 'Who the fuck are you, what you doing round here?' . . . there are, how can I say it, things taking place that people don't particularly want people knowing about or photographing. . . . [T]hose people sitting on the stoop, they don't want people in their faces photographing them. (1 April 2019)

In this case, striving to make hidden histories visible may also lead to injustices for local residents. In reimagining these everyday spaces of working-class life 'as tourist attractions', Jez was acutely aware that it came with a responsibility to ensure participants on the tour maintained a 'sensibility' when encountering the people in those spaces that 'they're living there, they're not to be gawked at' (1 April 2019). It is, therefore, important to consider the complexities of enacting cultural justice in terms of how storytelling about the past unfolds in contemporary lived spaces and how improving cultural justice outcomes for particular communities of interest might produce different forms of injustice for others.

3.3 Conclusion

Storytelling encourages the sharing of community knowledge and the contestation of singular or dominant 'official' histories that fail to acknowledge or recognise alternative narratives and interpretations that are valued by communities of interest. Although storytelling can take many forms, in this section we have focused on temporary exhibitions and permanent museum displays, tours and in situ markers. The examples we have drawn on highlight the extent to which the storytelling undertaken in music heritage initiatives presents connections between music and place that 'build upon, and contribute to, myths of popular music's past and its origin stories' (Baker et al., 2019, p. 56). For example, the emphasis in Birmingham on the Black Sabbath story – seen in this section in the dedicated temporary exhibition at BMAG and the WBID stars, bench and bridge – can work to elevate one aspect of Birmingham's popular music past at the expense of other more racially diverse experiences of popular music cultures (as highlighted by the minivan tour). Storytelling for cultural justice comes with a cautionary note: the overemphasis of 'the significance of a place in the cultural biography of an artist, genre or music scene' (Baker et al., 2019, p. 58) can 'replicate the dominant hegemonic versions of history' and diminish peoples' everyday experiences of popular music in place (Leonard, 2007, p. 156). However, the prominence of place in narratives of popular music's past can also advance the quest for cultural justice in the deindustrialising city, as was highlighted in the emphasis on education and elevating of marginalised histories in Exhibit 3000. The section has illustrated how the storying of music in the city can foster a sense of civic pride among local residents through the affirmation of the contribution of popular music to the cultural fabric of the city in ways that also signal to outsiders that the city's 'music culture is more diverse than is generally thought' (van der Hoeven & Brandellero, 2015, p. 48). Storytelling is a critical tool of cultural justice because the inclusion of diverse, marginalised voices highlights differentiated experiences that demonstrate the critical function that music holds for identity construction, politics of recognition and senses of place attachment.

4 Mobilising Communities for Collective Action

Effective and impactful popular music heritage initiatives require individuals and communities coming together for collective action. Community mobilisation may manifest as meetings, community consultation, workshops and symposia. For example, from 2014 to 2017, the DSC held annual conferences focused on bringing together academics, journalists, musicians, city officials, community workers and other industry personnel to discuss local popular music heritage projects and futures. Mobilising the community is also evident in the crowdsourcing of content or funds. The community group Friends of the Grande Ballroom, for instance, used the GoFundMe platform to raise money for the preservation of a significant Detroit rock music venue, including the funding of the Ballroom's building viability assessment in 2017 and emergency roof restoration in 2019. Direct activism and protest can also be components of this tool. Together, these varied activities enable the pooling of resources, sharing of knowledge and thinking through strategies aimed at generating social and cultural change.

The mobilisation of community emphasises participation, democratisation and the sharing of authority. Drawing on the literature on activist archiving and archival activism, we understand mobilisation to be a form of collective engagement in which 'the underlying motivation' for heritage projects resides in a desire to highlight 'inequity and injustice, with the intention of transforming the status quo' (Flinn & Sexton, 2019, p. 179). The possibility for cultural justice can be enhanced by attention to 'the power dynamics underpinning group participation' (Flinn & Sexton, 2019, p. 180). To illustrate this tool in action, we consider the approaches of the DSC, BMA and WAG, focusing on their nuanced approaches – stakeholder, do-it-together, participatory – to mobilising communities of interest. We end with a discussion of Sounds of Our Town, a research event that took place in October 2019 in Wollongong, which highlights our use of cultural justice as a method that supports community mobilisation and the development of supportive networks.

4.1 Detroit Sound Conservancy's Stakeholder Approach

As a grassroots heritage organisation with limited resources, the success of the DSC's projects has often been tied to their commitment to forge productive partnerships with multiple stakeholders. Carleton, the DSC's executive director at the time of our interview, was aware of the limitations of being a white man at the forefront of an organisation often working to conserve the music of African Americans in Black neighbourhoods. Taking a stakeholder approach to the DSC was therefore critical: 'I know what I look like . . . but my board, the majority are black, the co-founder's black' (Carleton, cited in Baker et al., 2020b, p. 36). The DSC's board of directors comprises people with varied skills and backgrounds – musicians, writers, an archivist, a historian, sound engineers, a judge and a grants and contracts administrator – who contribute their expertise to the organisation's functioning, decision-making and trajectory (see Detroit Sound Conservancy, 2020d). The diversity of the board members also provides the DSC with multiple entry points into the communities of interest the organisation seeks to work with. When Carleton stepped down as executive director of DSC in 2020, it was one of the Black board members who took his place: Michelle McKinney, an archivist and musician. Carleton highlighted the importance of this shift in leadership:

> With everything the city has gone through, there is not only a need to tell stories of struggle and justice and creative energy, there is also a demand for it. . . . That's why Michelle taking on this role is so important. She is African American, she is from the city, she has those community relationships, and that trust within the community. (cited in Wayne State University, 2021)

Community relationships and trust are central in the quest for cultural justice.

In addition to elevating the stories of Black communities, the DSC has also worked to preserve queer histories in Detroit, as demonstrated by their Club Heaven Sound System project. While Carleton is an ally, he acknowledged that it is queer board members who provide 'the direct, mainline connection into that community' (12 April 2019) and secure their support and involvement. From 1984 to 1994, Detroit's Club Heaven 'lay at the center of a civil rights struggle for LGBT youth struggling for a place . . . of their own within the whirlwind of the AIDS epidemic and ongoing discrimination' (Gholz, 2019). It was one of the many gay bars and clubs that had been operating in the city 'at the beginning of the AIDS crisis' (Gholz, 2019) but have since disappeared. In the case of Club Heaven, the site at 7 Mile and Woodward Avenue is now occupied by a fast-food restaurant. The DSC was 'gifted' the club's 'sound system by Detroit longtime techno producers, Derrick May and Kevin Saunderson' (Gholz, 2019) and the DSC then undertook an online crowdfunding campaign – yielding more than US$16,000 (Kickstarter, 2018) – to fund the restoration of this significant piece of Detroit's cultural history. Restoration of the sound system was undertaken by Audio Rescue Team, a business co-owned by DSC board member Michael Fotias. He said of the project:

> My intention is to restore it not to brand new, but the shape it was in when it was operating in the nightclub. . . . We want to respect the heritage of it as an artifact. . . . That place was important to so many walks of life and even though it's a sound system, it's the sound system from Heaven and that has a lot of bearings. A lot of those cats are still around. (cited in Zlatopolsky, 2017)

Multiple stakeholders have therefore been central to the early stages of this project. In addition to the crowdfunders, Derrick and Kevin, and the Audio Rescue Team, another stakeholder in the Club Heaven project is LGBT Detroit, the main 'community partner' who is working with DSC to bring attention to the ongoing fight against HIV/AIDS. Though many who originally experienced the Club Heaven Sound System survived, many did not. The first reported AIDS case in Detroit came just as Club Heaven first opened its doors. The impact of this disease has been devastating and continues to affect our community. DSC and LGBT Detroit will work together to create opportunities with the Sound System to bring awareness to this ongoing struggle. (Detroit Sound Conservancy, 2020b)

The preservation of popular music's heritage extends beyond the music itself, connecting to broader social and cultural moments in which the music was embedded. Taking action to restore the Club Heaven Sound System is, therefore, a springboard for telling important stories about Detroit's queer community that still resonate today. Undertaking this project in partnership with different stakeholders is crucial to ensuring these stories are told accurately and sensitively. By approaching heritage work in ways that engage multiple stakeholders, the DSC is able to draw on resources and expertise beyond their own organisation, build relationships with key communities of interest and cultural gatekeepers in the city and increase the visibility and impact of their work. Such an approach is mutually beneficial for the DSC, the organisations and individuals they partner with and the audiences they seek to engage.

4.2 Birmingham Music Archive's Do-It-Together Approach

Although it does not have a board like the DSC, the BMA similarly develops a collaborative approach to heritage that emphasises the 'collective work of building alternate popular music histories, heritage and archives' – what Jez (Collins, 2015, p. 84) labels a 'do-it-together' approach. In Section 2, we saw this approach in the extent to which Jez collects crowdsourced materials and memories in the spirit of democratising the city's popular music heritage. The BMA's do-it-together approach to heritage strategically fosters relationships with organisations and individuals at multiple points along the continuum of popular music heritage discourse, from unauthorised to authorised. In this way, the BMA can capture everyday experiences, ephemeral materials and marginalised voices and histories (see also discussion of Exhibit 3000 in Section 3) that may not typically be collected or preserved by mainstream heritage institutions. As a result, the BMA and its users are engaged in processes of public history-making – contributing to vernacular understandings of music and place – through collective uploading, 'exchanging and sharing of personal histories and knowledge' (Collins, 2015, p. 87).

In addition to connecting with communities of interest through crowdsourcing materials for the online archive, the BMA has forged partnerships with other local heritage practitioners and like-minded organisations in Birmingham to establish projects that have wider community reach, support and involvement. Although BMA was founded as an online archive, its activities have extended beyond collection and preservation, with the BMA involved in the curation of exhibitions such as '"Is There Anyone Out There?" Documenting Birmingham's Alternative Music Scene 1986–1990' (2016) at the Parkside Gallery and 'In the Que' (2022) at BMAG, as well as the production of documentaries including *Made in Birmingham: Reggae Punk Bhangra* (Collins & Shannon, 2010).

The 'Our Musical Roots' project, funded by the Heritage Lottery Fund, illustrates the BMA's networked approach to popular music heritage outreach and education. In 2016, the BMA – working alongside Birmingham-based arts company City of Colours (now Forward! Arts) – ran a ten-month long training programme for under-sixteens from underprivileged areas of Birmingham with an aim to explore and highlight the city's music heritage (Brookes et al., 2016, pp. 87–8). 'Our Musical Roots' sought 'to address a perceived "lack" of knowledge about the city's popular music heritage among younger members of the community, seeking to engender a sense of investment in its traditions and possibilities' and create a feeling of civic pride (Baker et al., 2020c, p. 45). A series of music heritage-focused workshops exposed the project participants to 'the breadth and diversity of the city's communities and its music: dub and reggae; bhangra and Asian produced; and metal and indie' (Baker et al., 2020c, p. 53). This involved a range of related activities including having the young people undertake 'interviews with musicians, investigate[] the city's iconic music venues and, in turn, share[] their knowledge and developing skills with other young people in heritage workshops organised in local schools' (Baker et al., 2020c, p. 53). Partners and participants in this project therefore expanded as the project rolled out, beginning with the non-profit arts organisations, to the initial group of under-sixteens, to the musicians interviewed and then the schools and their students. The potential for the project to reach more community members came by way of the project's legacy component: the creation of two large murals in inner-city suburbs of Birmingham which illustrated participants' new-found understanding of the city's music heritage. These murals act as another in situ marker (see Section 3) that not only signifies the importance of popular music heritage to Birmgingham's urban identity but also offers more opportunities for everyday engagement with the city's popular music past as residents and visitors move through those spaces. It is with partnerships like this that the BMA functions not just as a 'passive' archive or shrine to the past, but an active organisation that seeks to address contemporary inequalities through education and creative production.

In addition to working with other non-profit organisations (e.g. Vivid Projects, The Pump), the BMA actively reaches out to the for-profit sector to find ways in which developers, for example, might consider implementing popular music heritage initiatives in planning proposals. Jez explicitly describes this as a 'methodological approach to preserving Birmingham's music heritage through connecting and partnering with individuals, organisations, institutions and statutory bodies both local and regional' (Collins, 2020a, p. 14). For Jez, a do-it-together approach is not about setting out 'to be *the* voice of music heritage' (original emphasis) in Birmingham, but rather to 'advocate on behalf of the various actors in the sector and argue for more and better support; [to promote] the adoption of policies to protect, preserve and celebrate the city's heritage; and to harness the potential of this heritage and culture for economic, social and cultural benefits' (Collins, 2020a, p. 14).

In terms of built heritage, for instance, the BMA advocated for the preservation of parts of The Eagle and Tun, a pub in Birmingham with a strong connection to the reggae group UB40 (including as the venue where the Red Red Wine music video was filmed). The pub was slated to be one of many buildings in Birmingham demolished for the construction of a high speed rail line. The BMA worked to mobilise various partners, notably the railway developer and the Birmingham Museums Trust, to undertake 'an architectural salvage operation to save parts of the building' which can go on to be 'reconstructed for display and use in the Birmingham Museum & Art Gallery' (Collins, 2020a, p. 16). Such an example illustrates how the tools of cultural justice can overlap and intersect: in this instance, the BMA mobilised multiple stakeholders for the purposes of preserving a significant venue of Birmingham's popular music past.

Working with the for-profit sector has its challenges in a deindustrialising city undergoing continuous urban redevelopment. Jez expressed the struggle of getting property developers to understand how popular music heritage might have relevance to their agendas. Referencing the case of a company intending to build a hotel on the site of a prominent music venue in the city centre – The Crown, where Black Sabbath 'played their first ever gig' – Jez notes the BMA is 'trying to make that argument' to developers that 'Instead of just tearing it down . . . there are ways of incorporating it in, and that'll have benefits for you' (cited in Baker et al., 2020b, p. 13). Partnerships with developers involve communicating how a popular music heritage initiative will 'satisfy [their] economic needs' while also inviting them to 'stop and think about how you might do things differently' (cited in Baker et al., 2020b, p. 13). Jez's arguments in these negotiations are that the BMA provides 'a vehicle' for developers to 'give something back . . . and do some cultural good for the city' (1 April 2019). In this sense, Jez has the capacity to embed cultural justice principles into his partnerships, even if his for-profit partners do not hold cultural justice as a specific objective for their developments and even if such developments may be implicated in exacerbating injustices associated with gentrification. The examples of The Crown and The Eagle and Tun highlight the challenges in a quest for cultural justice. On the one hand, the potential for cultural justice outcomes are supported in terms of recognition of a community of interest's investment in the musical legacies of these heritage properties. On the other hand, the future impacts of development could potentially contribute to social forces like gentrification which have the capacity to introduce new forms of injustice in these neighbourhoods.

4.3 Wollongong Art Gallery's Participatory Approach

Wollongong Art Gallery, as a key cultural space in the city, hosts more than its collections of artworks, also programming talks, workshops and other events. WAG has a focus 'on visual art production' and 'visual art presentation', but, as the gallery's director John Monteleone explained, 'it's also a space for different types of creatives to come together and do things' (11 October 2018). From November 2014 to March 2015, WAG hosted the popular music heritage exhib- ition 'Steel City Sound'. John explained that he had long planned to hold an exhibition at WAG related to music, acknowledging that 'music is one of the ways in which creativity ferments within a working class town' like Wollongong (11 October 2018). In the process of looking for an expert on the music history of the Illawarra region, John came upon Warren's Steel City Sound website (see Section 2). Although Warren was not a professionally trained curator, he was hired by John as part of WAG's visiting curator programme to work on the Steel City Sound exhibition over an eighteen-month period, building on the content already established for the online archive.

Despite Warren's lack of 'professional' credentials in heritage, he was identified as a local expert in the exhibition's topic and was recognised as having the capacity to collect materials and create content that drew on the skills and networks he had built in his work as a public historian of Wollongong's popular music past. Indeed, Warren brought to the project 'a very strong vision', being 'so passionate and committed to the project' (John, 11 October 2018). John remarked that:

> Warren was essential ... if we didn't have Warren on board for the show, it
> would have been a very different type of exhibition. I don't think it would
> have had the level of depth and the passion involved. (11 October 2018)

The resulting exhibition was reflective of a participatory partnership between a DIY online archivist and a formal cultural institution, each 'acknowledge[ing] a diversity of expertise and operat[ing] from a premise of shared authority' (Roued-Cunliffe & Copeland, 2017, p. xv) in order to expand awareness of Wollongong's popular music heritage in ways that might not have occurred otherwise. This example highlights the value in bringing together the distinct resources and skillsets of authorised and self-authorised institutions and practices.

Within the participatory approach developed by WAG, Warren adopted a do-it-together approach to his role as curator for the exhibition, describing it as 'the result of the community coming together' to tell the story of the city's music history (12 October 2018). Many of the materials that appeared in the Steel City Sound exhibition were sourced from among the community. Warren put out calls for donated items on social media, local newspapers and his website, demonstrating the do-it-together intent driving his curatorship:

> This will be YOUR exhibition. This is your chance to display your memora-bilia, and tell us about your memories via audio and video recordings, photographs, flyers, set-lists, newspaper clippings, posters, t-shirts, stickers, etc. . . . Please have a think about what might be stored in your attics, cellars, back of the cupboards, under the beds, that you'd be willing to share and contribute to our history. (Wheeler, 2013b)

Here, Warren highlights the value of items in the hands of the community that may be seemingly mundane or taken-for-granted, but which have potential heritage value in their capacity to tell stories about the popular music of Wollongong. Such a collaboration can create opportunities to bring 'forgotten or overlooked histories' and objects 'to public attention for the first time' and enable a re-examination of the city's popular music and reappraisal of its cultural value (Leonard, 2015, p. 29). In addition to open calls, Warren directly contacted musicians and other relevant figures in his and WAG's networks. For instance, WAG put Warren in touch with Tom Dion, a photographer who had documented numerous Wollongong gigs, and Dave Curley, who ran music programmes at a local youth centre. The expansion of Warren's networks had a snowball effect that resulted in even more people getting involved in contrib-uting to the exhibition; as John explained, Warren's 'network grew bigger, and . . . people started to say, "I've got a photograph," and all of a sudden [the collection] started to grow' (11 October 2018).

Taking this participatory approach to heritage practitioner collaboration and do-it-together approach for engaging communities of interest in aspects of collection and curation enabled 'connections' and 'reconnections', with 'people coming together that hadn't seen each other for years' (Warren, 12 October 2018). Visitors to the exhibition were also invited to 'write little notes' featuring 'their own reminiscences or experiences' to add to a timeline of

Wollongong music-making featured on a wall of the gallery (John, 11 October 2018). The 'wall of notes' provided a space for remembrance and praise as well as voices of dissent. One attendee of the exhibition told us that they felt women's stories had been downplayed. They observed that the exhibition's narrative reflected the 'intense masculinity' of aspects of the city's broader music culture (Dune, 19 June 2019). In response to the exhibition being 'masculinist in its presentation', the participant described how 'a bunch of my friends and I wrote ... angry feminist messages' on stickers to leave behind on the wall of notes (Dune, 19 June 2019). Even exhibitions that are constructed through a do-it-together approach can reproduce dominant narratives. Gaps and silences may be due to those aspects on display having particularly 'effective and motivated supporters' (Leonard, 2015, p. 29), more material donated that relates to them, and/or greater alignment with curators' preferences, tastes and knowledge. It is also important to recognise, however, how these seemingly innocuous reasons for exclusions are underpinned by systemic forces and power dynamics that work to reinforce existing canons and downplay the contributions of marginalised groups. For instance, Reitsamer (2018) notes that women have come to be systemically excluded from popular music heritage projects partly due to discourses of 'historical importance' constructed by white male music critics and historians. These discourses have shaped how heritage values are understood and assigned and, subsequently, what comes to be collected, preserved and displayed. In the case of Steel City Sound, interactive components work to draw in more voices that can resist and offer correctives to the narratives the exhibition produces. WAG's 'wall of notes' provided an opportunity for the inclusion of counter-narratives – an extension of the collective action the participatory and do-it-together approaches of the exhibition had worked to establish.

Looking back on the exhibition, and reflecting on the participatory process, John commented that in the past people interested in Wollongong's music heritage had largely been operating in 'silos', acting 'on their own interest' (11 October 2018). Steel City Sound provided a space for musicians and others connected to Wollongong's music scenes to discover shared interests. John observed how 'one of the important things we found was that people like Warren ... got to meet these people, and started networking with them; and other musicians started to network with each other' (cited in Baker et al., 2020b, p. 31). Warren described 'the pleasures' he got from curating an exhibition which involved 'finding those people that are still around that were able to talk about the experiences and creating some strong friendships with people who I'd never otherwise ... have had contact with' (12 October 2018). As a result, a network was formed through the popular music heritage exhibition which could work to drive change in the city's contemporary music-making spheres: 'it became a real focal point at that time, to get music happening again, and a real interest in music in this area' (John, cited in Baker et al., 2020b, p. 31).

4.4 Sounds of Our Town: Mobilising as Method

As is apparent throughout this section, fieldwork for this project revealed the centrality of participation, partnerships and do-it-together approaches among popular music heritage initiatives in deindustrialising cities. In the interests of putting our conceptual framework of cultural justice into practice as a research method, we likewise sought to mobilise diverse stakeholders engaged in self-authorised and authorised heritage practice – including representatives from each case study city – to discuss the benefits, challenges and particularities of popular music heritage work in the context of industrial decline and urban revitalisation. In October 2019, we held a public panel, Sounds of Our Town, at WAG (see Figure 9). The panel brought together Carleton (DSC), Jez (BMA)

Figure 9 Panellists at the Sounds of Our Town public event held at WAG. From left to right: Professor Julianne Schultz (panel MC, Griffith University, Australia), Synnøve Engevik (Rockheim Museum, Trondheim, Norway), Jez Collins (BMA, UK), Daina Pocius (City of Playford, Australia), John Monteleone (WAG, Australia), Carolyn Laffan (Australian Music Vault, Australia), Dr Carleton Gholz (Detroit Sound Conservancy, USA). Photo by Zelmarie Cantillon

and John (WAG) as representatives of the case study cities, while also extending possibilities for comparison by including three heritage practitioners from other cities: Daina Pocius, Heritage Coordinator for City of Playford, South Australia, home to the deindustrialising locale of Elizabeth (best known for artists including Jimmy Barnes and Glenn Shorrock); Synnøve Engevik, Curator at Rockheim Museum, Norway, located in the deindustrialising city of Trondheim; and Carolyn Laffan, Curator at Australian Music Vault, Melbourne, which includes in its collection items from music scenes across the country, including deindustrialising cities like Newcastle, New South Wales and Geelong, Victoria (the former producing notable groups and musicians including Silverchair and The Screaming Jets, with the latter connected with the likes of Chrissy Amphlett and Magic Dirt). In addition to the public event, our time spent in Wollongong with the panellists involved informal discussions over lunches and dinners and scheduled activities for the research team and our international visitors (Jez and Carleton), including a tour of the steelworks and a collaborative zine-making session.

Chaired by Professor Julianne Schultz – author of *Steel City Blues* (1985), an account of one of Wollongong's harshest periods of industrial decline – questions posed to the panellists focused on their heritage projects, the impacts of deindustrialisation and new urban developments, the role of music in place-making, the influence of migration on music scenes, visitor/end-user engagement with heritage initiatives, working with local governments and the tensions between producing economic value and preserving cultural value. In their responses, panellists made links between the different cities, often pointing to contrasting experiences to signal their city's 'unique' qualities where people, music and the city intersect (Jez, cited in Baker et al., 2020b, p. 23). Responding to Carleton, for example, Jez pointed to differences between Birmingham and Detroit in terms of the start of the city's regeneration processes, the sociocultural characteristics of the population, the evolution of popular music and what was happening to the materials of popular music's past. Comparisons were also made in terms of approaches to heritage work in the cities represented by the panellists. As the chair of the panel observed, 'there's a pattern here that's emerging of people's active participation from the bottom up' (Julianne, cited in Baker et al., 2020b, p. 28). For example, Jez reflected on the Wollongong experience, synthesising what he had heard from other panellists and audience members to make a connection to his approach to safeguarding popular music heritage in Birmingham. John drew attention to the rich musical pasts of Detroit and Elizabeth to emphasise how Wollongong should keep focusing on popular music heritage to tell the city's story. Panellists also discussed experiences of working with governments for cultural projects and the relevance of popular music heritage in the present cultural life of these cities and for their future development. Speaking about the 'uphill struggle' in Birmingham, 'in terms of policy and strategy' and why local government 'should support music heritage' and 'contemporary music practices', Jez reflected 'I'm sure that's true in Detroit, and we were talking earlier, that it's probably the same in Australia, particularly in times of austerity' (cited in Baker et al., 2020b, p. 32). Jez's comments resonated with John in the context of Wollongong, who extended the observation by noting that the challenges are with 'governments of all stripes, whether federal, state or local', but prompted from Carolyn commentary that 'the experience in Melbourne has been quite different' (cited in Baker et al., 2020b, pp. 34–5).

Hearing from fellow panellists inspired Daina to launch a project through Playford Library to celebrate Elizabeth's popular music past: 'it was a fantastic opportunity to learn more about music history and Playford will definitely be doing more to preserve our music history' (email, 21 October 2019). The City of Playford encompasses thirty-five suburbs, including Elizabeth, an area north of Adelaide which developed in the mid-1950s as a satellite city to serve the car manufacturing industry. The restructuring and decline of this and other industries from the mid-1970s had severe consequences for the area, contributing to City of Playford being classified as the most disadvantaged area in the Adelaide Statistical Division (Australian Bureau of Statistics, 2013). The 2017 closure of the General Motors-Holden manufacturing plant – which had underpinned the area's economic base for decades – placed further strain on the community, producing major job losses for plant workers, component suppliers and service industries in the area (Beer et al., 2019; Browne-Yung et al., 2020). Holden had always loomed large in Elizabeth's identity and its closure posed a significant challenge to the economic vitality of the area and its social and cultural fabric. As with the other cities of our study, Elizabeth also had an interesting popular music past which could be drawn on to further reimage the area. Having experienced vibrant beat and pub rock scenes in the 1960s and 1970s influenced by British migrants, Elizabeth came to be called 'the cultural centre of rock music in Australia' (Beard cited in Zion, 1987, p. 2983). Daina observed that, with support of the local council, a contemporary music scene has developed in Elizabeth driven by 'African refugees, and they're the ones … creating the hip hop scene', with the area's community music hub 'creating some well-known hip hop artists' (cited in Baker et al., 2020b, p. 26). Drawing on the city's rich musical legacy, in November 2019, Daina put a call on the

Playford Library (2019) Facebook page announcing the heritage initiative 'Elizabeth: The Cradle of Rock':

> The City of Elizabeth quickly developed into a cultural centre of rock music in its early years. A number of bands and musicians began their musical journey in the dance hall atmosphere of Elizabeth. The City of Playford Library would like to celebrate the unsung heroes of the music scene, its artists, its listeners, its influence. If you have a story or memory to share, photographs, memorabilia of that period we would love for you to get in contact with us.

The Playford Library Facebook page published requests for community members to share their stories and memorabilia between November 2019 and March 2020, after which the COVID-19 pandemic disrupted the work of heritage institutions globally.

Panellists continued to engage in email exchanges proposing ways to maintain the network that had developed during the event. They reported returning to their home cities feeling 'very inspired' from the opportunity 'to hear how passionate you all are about the potential for music to transform your communities' (Carolyn, email, 19 October 2019). Panellists invited each other to be added to the mailing lists of their respective organisations so that they can 'stay in touch and continue to see and hear the work we do' (Carleton, email, 18 October 2019) and 'follow[] everyone's progress' (Jez, email, 24 October 2019). These email exchanges also provided greater insight into the heritage initiatives each was involved with beyond what could be discussed during our time together. For example, Synnøve shared the script of a talk she had delivered at a symposium, with her presentation expanding on the information provided during the panel. Panellists also provided links to playlists of music from their cities to further showcase the sounds of their town. Connections were further maintained by panellists following each other on Twitter. In some cases, there were opportunities for additional face-to-face meetings – some months after the panel, Carolyn gave Synnøve a tour of the Australian Music Vault and Australian Performing Arts Collection during a visit to Melbourne, leading Carolyn to note 'It feels like [the Sounds of Our Town panellists are] really starting to form a strong mutual support group' (email, 8 January 2020). These emerging networks, as well as Daina's establishment of a music heritage initiative in Playford, are evidence of the panel members' interest in discussing best practice for popular music heritage initiatives in deindustrialising cities and in the panel's capacity to mobilise action among those involved.

To extend the potential of cultural justice as method, the research team produced three zines during 2020, the year following the public panel. Zines 'serve as an apparatus for cultural justice' in that they 'have the capacity to act as community archive' (Baker & Cantillon, 2022). As a methodological tool, zines provide a publicly accessible and engaging space for researchers and participants to 'reflect on, discuss and resist' the experience of injustices (Baker & Cantillon, 2022). The first of the zines, *Sounds of Our Town: The Wollongong Edition* (Baker et al., 2020b), featured an editorial outlining the broader research project; brief definitions of key terms (e.g. cultural justice) for non-academic audiences; a transcription of a radio interview involving the research team, Jez and Carleton; a transcription of the public panel; and written pieces from Jez and Carleton reflecting on the connections between Wollongong and their own cities. Jez noted in his contribution that 'Growing up in Birmingham in the 1970s and 80s . . . it was apparent that the city was a tough, working class city, a place of people who pulled themselves up by the bootlaces and reinvented itself (particularly with the continual physical rebuilding of the city, something that continues to this day) and this has reminded me of Wollongong' (Collins, 2020b, p. 48). He observed how both cities share a similar narrative of the boom and bust of industry, the need of each city to 'look elsewhere to reinvent itself', a 'move[] towards the service sector' and a 'skyline . . . dominated with cranes building' developments which threaten live music venues (Collins, 2020b, p. 46). Carleton drew attention to similarities between the feeling of Port Kembla and locations in Michigan, writing:

> [T]he overall feeling was all too familiar. A little Delray, a little River Rouge, a little Hamtramck, . . . Detroit. These cities are uncomfortable because they don't lie. They have to be bulldozed to be forgotten or else they continue to be a reminder that the bosses don't have our best interests in mind, that this is not 'the best of all possible worlds'. (Gholz, 2020, p. 56)

A limited print run of zines were sent to sixteen cultural sites in Wollongong for distribution to be made freely available for people to pick up and read. This zine and its follow-up editions – *Sounds of Our Town: The Detroit Edition* (Baker et al., 2020a) and *Sounds of Our Town: The Birmingham Edition* (Buttigieg et al., 2020) – are available to download from the project website. Copies of the Detroit and Birmingham editions were also printed and sent to each of the panellists.

4.5 Conclusion

The work being undertaken by the DSC and BMA, and the contribution of WAG to the showcasing of Wollongong's popular music heritage, demonstrates how mobilisation of communities involves the distinct assets and expertise of multiple stakeholders. Working with a wide range of stakeholders – including communities of interest, community organisations, local governments and developers – can broaden available resources, foster productive partnerships and enhance the quality, reach and impact of heritage initiatives. Such an approach can cut across and draw together authorised, self-authorised and unauthorised heritage practices and institutions. While in this section we separated out three fields of activity – stakeholder, do-it-together, participatory – to tease apart the networking activities being undertaken in the cities of our study, in practice these are not truly separate, as is evident in the discussion of the Steel City Sound exhibition. Rather, these approaches provide different ways of thinking about community mobilisation in the pursuit of cultural justice. Michelle McKinney illustrates this well in reflecting on the operations of the DSC:

> [T]hey're actually going out into the neighborhoods, into the block clubs, going to the block club meetings, meeting the people who live in those neighborhoods and saying, 'well, how can we serve you? We're part of you, where we were growing out of the community, need to save this building, to save your legacy, to save your voice. This is our voice.' (cited in Detroit Sound Conservancy, 2019)

Cultural justice as a research method has similar goals, striving to connect with and mobilise different communities of interest in ways that can support their needs and bolster existing collective action.

5 Conclusion: A Critical Approach to Cultural Justice

In this Element, we have surveyed cultural justice as a lens through which to explore popular music heritage initiatives in deindustrialising cities. Our case studies of Detroit (USA), Birmingham (UK) and Wollongong (Australia) have highlighted how popular music heritage can be used to counter some of the injustices instigated or exacerbated by deindustrialisation. Our analysis of the case studies has also, however, revealed the ways in which cultural injustices may be perpetuated through heritage initiatives. This discussion has focused particularly on three tools that can be deployed in the (often complicated, sometimes fraught) quest for cultural justice: (1) collection, preservation and archiving; (2) curation, storytelling and heritage interpretation; and (3) mobilising communities for collective action. In this final section, we touch on a number of obstacles that can hamper the quest for cultural justice in heritage initiatives focused on popular music. We then detail key components for a cultural justice toolkit, offering a preliminary set of guiding principles for heritage practitioners and scholars seeking to take a cultural justice approach to heritage.

5.1 A Critical Cultural Justice Lens

Not all popular music heritage initiatives are inherently aligned with a cultural justice approach or able to activate the cultural justice potentials of popular music's past. Although creative strategies for urban revitalisation and community renewal are frequently drawn on by different levels of government to help combat the deleterious effects of deindustrialisation, these strategies are often 'top-down' approaches, such as cultural policy schemes developed and implemented by local governments in partnership with consultants and property developers. Rather than working towards cultural justice, government-sanctioned creative city strategies can contribute to the further marginalisation and displacement of already disenfranchised groups. Such strategies can amplify the non-recognition and disrespect of cultural identities and histories and, subsequently, contribute to the deterioration of civic pride and place attachment. When economic imperatives are prioritised over social and cultural vitality, the risk for marginalisation and displacement is intensified. Indeed, even grassroots, DIY heritage initiatives may resist particular injustices for some communities of interest while reinforcing various injustices for others.

Further challenges to cultural justice can be encountered in relation to labour conditions whereby organisations and institutions, perhaps sometimes unknowingly, reproduce traditional internal hierarchies or other exclusionary work practices. For instance, injustices can be enacted via extractivist working environments; unsafe working conditions; bullying, discrimination and harassment; a homogenous workforce that underrepresents marginalised groups and communities of interest; and failing to accommodate staff or volunteers with disabilities, neurodivergence, caring responsibilites and so on. Indeed, the emphasis in many initiatives on volunteering could itself be perceived as perpetuating injustices. While volunteering for heritage projects can bring substantial rewards, it is not without its costs. The drawbacks of volunteering can be financial, but can also manifest as tensions that are relational, temporal, interpersonal, emotional and physical (see Cantillon & Baker, 2020). Moreover, when participation in popular music heritage projects relies on unpaid labour, it can exclude those who are not in a financial position to give their time, which, in turn, could result in certain voices and perspectives being silenced. The issue of unpaid labour is of particular concern for those projects in which economic value is being created for the heritage sector on the back of a largely volunteer workforce. Injustices connected to the reliance on volunteers and their gifting of labour is perhaps heightened in the context of the deindustrialising city, where there may be limited opportunities for paid employment. The quest for cultural justice, then, is as much about the labour practices involved in heritage projects as it is about the products of that labour.

A cultural justice lens is valuable in its ability to illuminate the productive contributions of heritage initiatives to tackling the effects of cultural injustices. However, a *critical* approach to cultural justice is necessary to uncover those elements of heritage initiatives that perpetuate injustices. Such an approach draws attention to, for example, the predilection to celebrate the stories of white men to the detriment of marginalised groups, as was indicated in regard to the 'Black Sabbath – 50 Years' exhibition (see Section 3), or ignoring and downplaying the contributions and experiences of women, as was touched on in the discussion of the Steel City Sound exhibition (see Section 4). Revealing the harmful or problematic aspects of heritage initiatives paves the way for heritage practitioners to continue working on and addressing those issues as they move forward in their quest for cultural justice. For instance, while some of the most prominent examples discussed in this Element were founded by white men – Jez and the BMA, Carleton and the DSC – it is also clear that these individuals are continually exercising reflexivity surrounding their positionality within their local contexts and heritage work, actively trying to approach their initiatives in ways that are more inclusive.

For heritage practitioners involved in creating initiatives to preserve popular music's past, a critical cultural justice lens can be enlisted to cultivate cultural justice outcomes in their projects. The previous sections highlight that the cultural justice potentials of popular music heritage are most evident in initiatives that draw connections between music and broader social, cultural, economic and historical circumstances, such as the links between Black creativity and techno in Exhibit 3000 (see Section 3) or the potential of popular music heritage to combat social exclusion of young people in Birmingham (see Section 4). Popular music heritage initiatives should also seek to be inclusive of multiple (sometimes conflicting) voices and perspectives, as well as representing difficult heritage instead of just celebratory narratives. Similarly, popular music heritage projects should be attentive to the contestations, uncertainties and tensions that constitute the communities (of interest, of locality or of other identities) they seek to represent – efforts we saw in Jez's concerns about his music tours in Birmingham (see Section 3) and Carleton's reflections on the work being undertaken in Detroit to preserve the Blue Bird Inn (see Section 2). Working with a critical cultural justice lens can enable heritage practitioners, as well as scholars, to purposefully incorporate some of these dissonances and interconnections that constitute communities, cities and histories as complex and shifting assemblages.

It is also crucial for scholars and practitioners to recognise that cultural justice is not something fixed that can necessarily be 'achieved', but an ongoing process. This processual quality is captured in Jez's reflections on how the BMA's digital archive might be developed in the future to more fully represent people's experiences and memories of that city's popular music past (see Section 2). The processual quality of cultural justice is also observed in the

DSC's recognition that the quest for cultural justice does not end with the restoration of the Club Heaven Sound System, but rather consists of an ongoing partnership with LGBT Detroit to enlist the artefact for AIDS education (see Section 4). In the pursuit of cultural justice, heritage practitioners need to be sensitive and open to issues that arise around power, participation, access and representation in their projects. Cultural justice is most likely to be experienced in popular music heritage initiatives that embrace multiple, intersectional narratives surrounding the cultural expressions, people and places being documented.

5.2 The Cultural Justice Toolkit

In cultural policymaking, toolkits have become a staple for providing an evidence base to measure the socio-economic impacts of arts and culture initiatives, especially in urban contexts. Belfiore and Bennett (2010, p. 122) describe a 'toolkit mentality' among 'politicians, civil servants, arts funders, cultural administrators' who desire 'a straightforward method of impact evaluation, easily replicable in different geographical contexts and equably applicable to different art forms and diverse audiences'. These authors note that the 'toolkit approach' is problematic in that it provides 'excessive simplifications' as well as reflecting tendencies towards the uncurbed 'instrumentalization' of cultural life (Belfiore & Bennett, 2010, p. 122). We offer the cultural justice toolkit not as a set of criteria to formally assess the value of heritage initiatives or organisations, or as an exhaustive or fixed set of procedures, but rather as a series of open-ended guiding principles that can be used to shape the design and analysis of heritage initiatives. Although we discussed the tools separately in the preceding sections, here we present the items of the toolkit together as a way to emphasise that the tools of cultural justice are interconnected and overlapping. Instead of a direct application of tools, we hope the following principles invite critical thinking, inquiry and dialogue around the key issues of power, participation, access, representation and impact that manifest in different ways according to the specificity of the heritage initiatives, communities of interest and urban contexts in question. We invite others to expand on and investigate the following aims, approaches and considerations further. This is not a box-ticking exercise; a commitment to cultural justice is about intent, action, listening, reflection and adjustment, not fulfilling a predefined set of criteria.

1. The collection, archiving and display of popular music heritage should be underpinned by a *commitment to accessibility*. This commitment encompasses providing a 'space for community participation', where people can

'share' their memories, feelings and experiences without fearing that contributions might be 'wrong' (Jez, 1 April 2019). It also involves ensuring that collections are, to some degree, accessible to the public – so that archival material is not only being preserved but is also available to be consulted and used (for research, education, family histories, creative practice, consultations, etc).

2. Acknowledging that history resides in people, the collection of popular music heritage should aim to *capture diverse voices, identities, expressions and experiences* in the archive so that a plurality of engagements with popular music in the city can be represented in the present and preserved for future generations.

3. The recognition of material and symbolic significance should extend beyond the archive to encompass *actions to safeguard built heritage* in ways that recognise and reinterpret these spaces as lived heritage sites.

4. The preservation of built heritage needs to be done in *genuine consultation with residents and communities of interest* in ways that acknowledge 'historical hurt' (Carleton, 12 April 2019) and contemporary socio-economic conditions.

5. Storytelling should strive to *reinstate dignity and respect through education*, providing narratives that 'transform negative stereotypes' (Adam, 7 September 2019).

6. Interpretive panels and tour narration must be *rich in contextualisation*, providing detailed stories that recognise the complex experiences of the people and cultures being represented.

7. Storytelling must be *sensitive to cultural diversity* to ensure that in doing justice to one aspect of a city's heritage, the narration does not subsequently reinforce other aspects of cultural domination. It is essential to consider gender, class, race, ethnicity, age, sexuality and disability when elevating hidden histories so as to avoid new forms of myth-making that reproduce the non-recognition or misrecognition of others' stories.

8. Initiatives should work to *build community relationships and develop trust* from the outset through an emphasis on partnerships which can harness pre-existing networks and activate vernacular knowledge, skills and expertise.

9. A focus on *outreach activities* can work to continually expand networks, develop new partnerships and enhance possibilities for further collective action.

10. Organisations need to *foster an inclusive environment for participation* that invites different voices and perspectives.

11. Heritage practitioners should be prepared to *work with partners* who do not necessarily share the same mission or objectives but can offer valuable resources and networks to support heritage projects oriented towards cultural justice.

12. Initiatives are ideally underpinned by an aim to *build community* in a way that will 'add value to people's lives' (John, 11 October 2018) and their well-being through an emphasis on 'inclusivity' (Jez, 6 September 2019) and 'respect' (Julie, 9 October 2018) that provides locals with a 'sense of "this is our place"' (Ashley, 9 October 2018).

13. There should be a focus on *embedding education* as a guiding principle in popular music heritage activities in ways that will develop cultural competencies and support the activation of creativity in the next generation.

14. Practitioners should consider how their initiatives can *cultivate civic pride* in ways that will celebrate the community's 'common ground' (James, 12 October 2018), promoting a feeling of belonging (Aaron, 9 October 2018) and 'community identity' (Joel, 5 April 2019).

15. Beyond the focus on popular music's past, heritage initiatives should have a broader objective of *working toward social change*. Such a task requires dialogues and education about 'socially relevant issues' from the past and in the present (John, 12 April 2019), including 'systemic racism' and other 'isms' like sexism and ageism (Michelle, 8 April 2019) that have impacted a community's well-being, livelihood and their creativity.

16. Activating social and cultural change through education necessitates popular music heritage initiatives *speak to a broader public* (John, 11 October 2018) beyond 'niche' communities of interest (Bill, 3 September 2019), ensuring messages are outward focused at the same time that they speak directly to and reflect the experiences of those whose histories are being represented.

These aims, approaches and considerations for a cultural justice approach to heritage practice can also inform scholarly work on music, heritage and the city that seek to adopt a critical cultural justice lens conceptually and methodologically. The aforementioned principles can provide points of analytical focus for research that explores the three key fields of heritage practice that have been identified in the Element: collection, preservation and archiving; curation, storytelling and heritage interpretation; and mobilising communities for collective action. When embedding cultural justice methodologically, researchers are encouraged to consider how communities of interest can be involved in participatory research processes and to explore methods that might contribute to more culturally just outcomes for those being researched. Consideration might also be given to how data analysis and writing up might be done in ways that recognise and reflect the diversity of participant identities and experiences. Such an orientation involves the adoption of scholarly language that is attuned to the dignity of the communities being examined and which works against reproducing experiences of non-recognition or misrecognition. A concern for the accessibility of research findings and scholarly outputs is also important, particularly in terms of ensuring research speaks to a broader public beyond the academy.

Again, we stress that the aforementioned principles are prompts for thinking and acting in more culturally just ways. Even if an initiative were to take into account all of the items listed, cultural justice would not by default be 'achieved'. Cultural justice is a process that involves continuous effort and engagement with different stakeholders, attending to their specific (and some-times conflicting) needs, desires and interests. We recognise there are systemic, structural challenges which constrain the capacity for any individual or organ-isation to enact cultural justice through heritage work or scholarship. What is needed is action at all levels of government to implement cultural policy and cultural infrastructure strategies that can address the resource challenges and institutional pressures encountered by heritage practitioners (both in DIY and authorised settings) so that they are adequately supported in the quest for cultural justice. Without this shift, the heritage sector will continue to face largely insurmountable hurdles in relation to sustainability, threatening to undo the work of cultural justice that has been pursued to date. In the meantime, the guiding principles of a critical cultural justice approach offer practitioners and scholars a way forward in prioritising the potential of heritage to contribute to more just cities and societies.

References

Andres, L. & Chapain, C. (2013). The integration of cultural and creative industries into local and regional development strategies in Birmingham and Marseille: Towards an inclusive and collaborative governance? *Regional Studies*, 47(2), 161–82.

Australian Bureau of Statistics (2013). *New Data from the 2011 Census Reveals South Australia's Most Advantaged and Disadvantaged Areas.* www.abs.gov .au/ausstats/abs@.nsf/Lookup/by%20Subject/2033.0.55.001~2011~Media %20Release~2011%20Census%20(SEIFA)%20for%20Adelaide%20 (Media%20Release)~6.

Australian Bureau of Statistics (2017). *2016 Census QuickStats: Wollongong (Urban Centres and Localities)*. https://quickstats.censusdata.abs.gov .au/census_services/getproduct/census/2016/quickstat/UCL102005?open document.

Baird, M. F. (2014). Heritage, human rights, and social justice. *Heritage & Society*, 7(2), 139–55.

Baker, S. (2018). *Community Custodians of Popular Music's Past: A DIY Approach to Heritage.* London: Routledge.

Baker, S. & Cantillon, Z. (2022). Zines as community archive. *Archival Science*, 22, 539–61.

Baker, S., Cantillon, Z. & Buttigieg, B. (eds.) (2020a). *Sounds of Our Town: The Detroit Edition.* www.soundsofourtown.com/_files/ugd/8a61d6_1bf1f2c19e 4647bf9868354be01dd8f0.pdf.

Baker, S., Cantillon, Z. & Nowak, R. (eds.) (2020b). *Sounds of Our Town: The Wollongong Edition.* https://acf72f70-710a-40b9-92db-5b7934011262.file susr.com/ugd/8a61d6_ad6e94c88a4847dd8d003004a36224ae.pdf.

Baker, S. & Collins, J. (2015). Sustaining popular music's material culture in community archives and museums. *International Journal of Heritage Studies*, 21(10), 983–96.

Baker, S., Istvandity, L. & Nowak, R. (2019). *Curating Pop: Exhibiting Popular Music in the Museum.* New York: Bloomsbury.

Baker, S., Nowak, R., Long, P., Collins, J. & Cantillon, Z. (2020c). Community well-being, post-industrial music cities and the turn to popular music heritage. In C. Ballico & A. Watson, eds., *Music Cities: Evaluating a Global Cultural Policy Concept.* Cham: Palgrave Macmillan, pp. 43–62.

Ballico, C. & Watson, A. (2020). Introduction. In C. Ballico & A. Watson, eds., *Music Cities: Evaluating a Global Cultural Policy Concept*. Cham: Palgrave Macmillan, pp. 1–18.

Banerjee, D. & Steinberg, S. L. (2015). Exploring spatial and cultural discourses in environmental justice movements. *Journal of Rural Studies*, 39, 41–50.

Banks, M. (2017). *Creative Justice: Cultural Industries, Work and Inequality*. New York: Rowman & Littlefield.

Barber, A. & Hall, S. (2008). Birmingham: Whose urban renaissance? Regeneration as a response to economic restructuring. *Policy Studies*, 29(3), 281–92.

Barnes, K., Waitt, G., Gill, N. & Gibson, C. (2006). Community and nostalgia in urban revitalisation: A critique of urban village and creative class strategies as remedies for social 'problems'. *Australian Geographer*, 37(3), 335–54.

Bastian, J. A. & Alexander, B. (2009). Introduction: Communities and archives – a symbiotic relationship. In J. A. Bastian & B. Alexander, eds., *Community Archives: The Shaping of Memory*. London: Facet, pp. xxi–xxiv.

Beer, A., Weller, S., Barnes, T. et al. (2019). The urban and regional impacts of plant closures. *Regional Studies*, 6(1), 380–94.

Belfiore, E. & Bennett, O. (2010). Beyond the 'toolkit approach': Arts impact evaluation research and the realities of cultural policy-making. *Journal for Cultural Research*, 14(2), 121–42.

Bell, D. (1999). *The Coming of Post-industrial Society*. New York: Basic Books.

Birmingham City Council (2012). *Destination Birmingham: Birmingham, a Music City – A Report from Overview & Scrutiny*. www.birmingham.gov .uk/download/downloads/id/450/destination_birmingham_a_music_city_ february_2012.pdf.

Birmingham City Council (2019). *Birmingham Update January 2019*. www .birmingham.gov.uk/download/downloads/id/4780/birmingham_update_ january_2019.pdf.

Birmingham City Council (2021). *Mid-2020 Mid-year Population Estimates*. https://www.birmingham.gov.uk/download/downloads/id/9854/2020_mid-year_population_estimate.pdf

Birmingham Music Archive (n.d.). *About Us*. www.birminghammusicarchive .com/about-us/.

Bottà, G. (2015). Dead industrial atmosphere: Popular music, cultural heritage and industrial cities. *Journal of Urban Cultural Studies*, 2(1–2), 107–19.

Briller, S. & Sankar, A. (2013). Engaging opportunities in urban revitalization: Practicing Detroit anthropology. *Annals of Anthropological Practice*, 37(1), 156–78.

Brook, O., O'Brien, D. & Taylor, M. (2020). *Culture Is Bad for You: Inequality in the Cultural and Creative Industries*. Manchester: Manchester University Press.

Brookes, N., Kendall, J. & Mitton, L. (2016). Birmingham, priority to economics, social innovation at the margins. In T. Brandsen, S. Cattacin, A. Evers & A. Zimmer, eds., *Social Innovations in the Urban Context*. London: Springer Open, pp. 83–96.

Browne-Yung, K., Ziersh, A., Baum, F., Friel, S. & Spoehr, J. (2020). General Motor Holden's closure in Playford, South Australia: Analysis of the policy response and its implications for health. *Australian Journal of Public Administration*, 79(1), 76–92.

Burch-Brown, J. (2020). Should slavery's statues be preserved? On transitional justice and contested heritage. *Journal of Applied Philosophy*, 39, 807–24. https://doi.org/10.1111/japp.12485.

Burling, N. (dir.) (2012). *The Occy: A Doco*. Wollongong: Go Vegan Films.

Buttigieg, B., Cantillon, Z. & Baker, S. (eds.) (2020). *Sounds of Our Town: The Birmingham Edition*. www.soundsofourtown.com/_files/ugd/8a61d6_004867ff143d471a9daa8df986ac1c44.pdf.

Byrne, D. (2008). Heritage as social action. In J. Fairclough, R. Harrison, J. H. Jameson & J. Schofield, eds., *The Heritage Reader*. London: Routledge, pp. 149–73.

Çağlar, A. & Schiller, N. D. (2018). *Migrants & City-Making: Dispossession, Displacement, and Urban Regeneration*. Durham: Duke University Press.

Cantillon, Z. (2022). Urban reimaging, heritage and the making of a world-class city: The Commonwealth Walkway as mega-event legacy project. *Heritage & Society*. https://doi.org/10.1080/2159032X.2022.2127177.

Cantillon, Z. & Baker, S. (2020). Serious leisure and the DIY approach to heritage: Considering the costs of career volunteering in community archives and museums. *Leisure Studies*, 39(2), 266–79.

Cantillon, Z., Baker, S. & Buttigieg, B. (2017). Queering the community music archive. *Australian Feminist Studies*, 32(91–92), 41–57.

Cantillon, Z., Baker, S. & Nowak, R. (2021a). A cultural justice approach to popular music heritage in deindustrialising cities. *International Journal of Heritage Studies*, 27(1), 73–89.

Cantillon, Z., Baker, S. & Nowak, R. (2021b). Music heritage, cultural justice and the Steel City: Archiving and curating popular music history in Wollongong, Australia. In L. Maloney & J. Schofield, eds., *Music and*

Heritage: New Perspectives on Place-Making and Sonic Identity. London: Routledge, pp. 103–13.

Capsule (2019a). Hippy flower power. *Black Sabbath – 50 Years* exhibition. Birmingham: Birmingham Museum & Art Gallery, 12 September.

Capsule (2019b). Humble beginnings. *Black Sabbath – 50 Years* exhibition. Birmingham: Birmingham Museum & Art Gallery, 12 September

Capsule (2019c). Iommi's missing finger. *Black Sabbath – 50 Years* exhibition. Birmingham: Birmingham Museum & Art Gallery, 12 September.

Capsule (2019d). The press hated us. *Black Sabbath – 50 Years* exhibition. Birmingham: Birmingham Museum & Art Gallery, 12 September.

Capsule (2020). *About*. www.capsule.org.uk/about/.

Cele, S. (2021). Communicating back: Reflections on IBZM as participatory dissemination – commentary on Valli. *Fennia*, 199(1), 136–8.

Che, D. (2007). Connecting the dots to urban revitalization with the Heidelberg project. *Material Culture*, 39(1), 33–49.

Che, D. (2008). Sports, music, entertainment and the destination branding of post-Fordist Detroit. *Tourism Recreation Research*, 33(2), 195–206.

Che, D. (2009). Techno: Music and entrepreneurship in post-Fordist Detroit. In O. Johansson & T. Bell, eds., *Sound, Society and the Geography of Popular Music*. Burlington: Ashgate, pp. 261–7.

Chynoweth, A., Lynch, B., Peterson, K. & Smed, S. (eds.) (2021). *Museums and Social Change*. London: Routledge.

City of Detroit (2019). *Final Report: Proposed Blue Bird Inn Historic District, 5021 Tireman Street*. Detroit: Historic Designation Advisory Board. https://detroitmi.gov/sites/detroitmi.localhost/files/2020-12/Blue%20Bird%20Inn%20HD%20final%20report.pdf.

Clark, A. (2020). Reviving Detroit's historic Blue Bird Inn. *Belt Magazine*, 22 May. https://beltmag.com/detroit-blue-bird-inn-revival-restoration-jazz/.

Collins, J. (2015). Doing-it-together: Public history making and activist archivism in online popular music archives. In S. Baker, ed., *Preserving Popular Music Heritage*. New York: Routledge, pp. 77–90.

Collins, J. (2020a). Collecting, preserving and storying Birmingham's popular music heritage. In B. Buttigieg, Z. Cantillon & S. Baker, eds., *Sounds of Our Town: The Birmingham Edition*. Parramatta, NSW: Sounds of Our Town, pp. 5–21. https://acf72f70-710a-40b9-92db-5b7934011262.filesusr.com/ugd/8a61d6_004867ff143d471a9daa8df986ac1c44.pdf.

Collins, J. (2020b). Jez Collins' potted history of Birmingham, its music and the Birmingham Music Archive's connection to Steel City Sound. In S. Baker, Z. Cantillon & R. Nowak, eds., *Sounds of Our Town: The Wollongong Edition*. Parramatta, NSW: Sounds of Our Town, pp. 48–50. https://

acf72f70-710a-40b9-92db-5b7934011262.filesusr.com/ugd/8a61d6_ad6e94
c88a4847dd8d003004a36224ae.pdf.

Collins, J. & Shannon R. (dir.) (2010). *Made in Birmingham: Reggae Punk Bhangra*. Birmingham: Swish Film Production.

Cvetkovich, A. (2003). *An Archive of Feelings: Trauma, Sexuality and Lesbian Public Cultures*. Durham: Duke University Press.

Cwiek, S. (2019). Detroit's historic United Sound Systems studio spared from demolition. *Michigan Radio*, 11 January. www.michiganradio.org/arts-culture/2019-01-11/detroits-historic-united-sound-systems-studio-spared-from-demolition.

Denning, M. (2004). *Culture in the Age of Three Worlds*. London: Verso.

DeNora, T. (2000). *Music in Everyday Life*. Cambridge: Cambridge University Press.

Detroit Sound Conservancy (2019). *Preserving and Archiving Detroit's Black History: Discussion*. http://detroitsound.org/artifact/preserving-black-history/.

Detroit Sound Conservancy (2020a). *Blue Bird Stage*. http://detroitsound.org/blue-bird-stage/.

Detroit Sound Conservancy (2020b). *Club Heaven Sound System*. http://detroitsound.org/heaven/.

Detroit Sound Conservancy (2020c). *United Sound Systems*. http://detroitsound.org/unitedsound/.

Detroit Sound Conservancy (2020d). *Who We Are*. http://detroitsound.org/about/who-we-are/.

Detroit Sound Conservancy (2021a). *The Legendary Blue Bird Inn: Placekeeping a Community Resource on Tireman Avenue*. http://detroitsound.org/5021tireman/.

Detroit Sound Conservancy (2021b). *Vision, Mission and Goals*. http://detroitsound.org/mission/.

Detroit Sound Conservancy (2022). *Grant Announcement: DSC Awarded KIP: D+ $150,000 for Blue Bird Inn Rehabilitation*. http://detroitsound.org/grant-announcement-dsc-awarded-kipd-150000-for-blue-bird-inn-rehabilitation/5021-tireman/2022/.

Doucet, B. (2020). Deconstructing dominant narratives of urban failure and gentrification in a racially unjust city: The case of Detroit. *Tijdschrift voor economische en sociale geografie*, 111(4), 634–51.

Doucet, B. & Smit, E. (2016). Building an urban 'renaissance': Fragmented services and the production of inequality in Greater Downtown Detroit. *Journal of Housing and the Built Environment*, 31, 635–57.

Drury, C. (2021). A city on the brink? Birmingham facing 'disaster' as unemployment hits levels not seen since Eighties. *The Independent*, 21 March. www.independent.co.uk/news/uk/home-news/a-city-on-the-brink-birmingham-facing-disaster-as-unemployment-hits-levels-not-seen-since-eighties-b1818927.html.

Duff, W. M., Flinn, A., Suurtamm, K. E. & Wallace, D. A. (2013). Social justice impact of archives: A preliminary investigation. *Archival Science*, 13(4), 317–48.

Eisinger, P. (2014). Is Detroit dead? *Journal of Urban Affairs*, 36(1), 1–12.

Exhibit 3000 (2020). *Exhibit 3000: Detroit Techno Museum*. https://exhibit3000.com.

Fairchild, C. (2021). *Musician in the Museum: Display and Power in Neoliberal Popular Culture*. New York: Bloomsbury.

Feeley, D. (2016). Detroit: Realities of destructive accumulation. *Alternate Routes: A Journal of Critical Social Research*, 27, 300–12.

Filippucci, P. (2009). Heritage and methodology: A view from social anthropology. In M. L. S. Sørensen & J. Carman, eds., *Heritage Studies: Methods and Approaches*. London: Routledge, pp. 319–25.

Flinn, A. (2007). Community histories, community archives: Some opportunities and challenges. *Journal of the Society of Archivists*, 28(2), 151–76.

Flinn, A. (2011). Archival activism: Independent and community-led archives, radical public history and the heritage professions. *InterActions: UCLA Journal of Education and Information Studies*, 7(2), 1–20.

Flinn, A. & Sexton, A. (2019). Activist participatory communities in archival contexts: Theoretical perspectives. In E. Benoit III & A. Eveleigh, eds., *Participatory Archives: Theory and Practice*. London: Facet, pp. 173–90.

Flinn, A. & Stevens, M. (2009). 'It is noh mistri, wi mekin histri'. Telling our own story: Independent and community archives in the UK, challenging and subverting the mainstream. In J. A. Bastian & B. Alexander, eds., *Community Archives: The Shaping of Memory*. London: Facet, pp. 3–28.

Florida, R. (2002). *The Rise of the Creative Class*. New York: Basic Books.

Florida, R. & Adler, P. (2018). The patchwork metropolis: The morphology of the divided postindustrial city. *Journal of Urban Affairs*, 40(5), 609–24.

Fraser, N. (1995). From redistribution to recognition? Dilemmas of justice in a 'post-socialist' age. *New Left Review*, 212, 68–93.

Fraser, E. (2018). Unbecoming place: Urban imaginaries in transition in Detroit. *Cultural Geographies*, 25(3), 441–58.

Gentry, K. & Smith, L. (2019). Critical heritage studies and the legacies of the late-twentieth century heritage canon. *International Journal of Heritage Studies*, 25(11), 1148–68.

Ghaddar, J. J. & Caswell, M. (2019). 'To go beyond': Towards a decolonial archival praxis. *Archival Science*, 19, 71–85.

Gholz, C. (2011). 'Where the mix is perfect': Voices from the post-Motown soundscape. Unpublished PhD Thesis, University of Pittsburgh. http://d-scholarship.pitt.edu/7337/1/GholzDissMay2011.pdf.

Gholz, C. (2019). Magic, liberation, and architecture: Placekeeping musical space in Detroit. *Paprika!*, 5(2). https://yalepaprika.com/folds/the-architectural-gaze-goes-clubbing/magic-liberation-and-architecture-placekeeping-musical-space-in-detroit.

Gholz, C. (2020). From Waawiiyatanong to Mt. Keira: Popular music impressions from #SoundsOfOurTown. In S. Baker, Z. Cantillon & R. Nowak, eds., *Sounds of Our Town: The Wollongong Edition*. Parramatta, NSW: Sounds of Our Town, pp. 51–57. https://acf72f70-710a-40b9-92db-5b7934011262.file susr.com/ugd/8a61d6_ad6e94c88a4847dd8d003004a36224ae.pdf.

Gibson, C. (2013). Welcome to Bogan-ville: Reframing class and place through humour. *Journal of Australian Studies*, 37(1), 62–75.

Gibson, C., Brennan-Horley, C., Laurenson, B. et al. (2012). Cool places, creative places? Community perceptions of cultural vitality in the suburbs. *International Journal of Cultural Studies*, 15(3), 287–302.

Goldberg-Miller, S. B. D. (2019). Creative city strategies on the municipal agenda in New York. *City, Culture and Society*, 17, 26–37.

Gonda, J. D. (2015). *Unjust Deeds: The Restrictive Covenant Cases and the Making of the Civil Rights Movement*. Chapel Hill: University of North Carolina Press.

Greater Birmingham Chambers of Commerce (2018a). *Birmingham Economic Review 2018 – Chapter 2: People*. www.birmingham.ac.uk/Documents/college-social-sciences/business/research/city-redi/birmingham-economic-review-2018/ber-2018-ch-2-people.pdf.

Greater Birmingham Chambers of Commerce (2018b). *Birmingham Economic Review 2018 – Summary*. www.sportbirmingham.org/uploads/chamber-economic-review-2018.pdf.

Grodach, C., Foster, N. & Murdoch, J. (2018). Gentrification, displacement and the arts: Untangling the relationship between arts industries and place change. *Urban Studies*, 55(4), 807–25.

Hagan, J. (2002). Epilogue, 1980–2001. In J. Hagan & H. Lee, eds., *A History of Work and Community in Wollongong*. Rushcutters Bay: Halstead Press, pp. 163–79.

Hagan, J. & Lee, H. (2002). Part I: The making of community, 1880–1940: Introduction. In J. Hagan & H. Lee, eds., *A History of Work and Community in Wollongong*. Rushcutters Bay: Halstead Press, pp. 3–7.

Harrison, L. M. (2010). Factory music: How the industrial geography and working-class environment of post-war Birmingham fostered the birth of heavy metal. *Journal of Social History*, 44(1), 145–58.

Hennion, A. (2007). Those things that hold us together: Taste and sociology. *Cultural Sociology*, 1(1), 97–114.

Herstad, K. (2017). 'Reclaiming' Detroit: Demolition and deconstruction in the Motor City. *The Public Historian*, 39(4), 85–113.

Herstad, K. (2019). 'The eternal drabness of DeHoCo': Documenting and memorializing built heritage through urban exploration in Detroit. In J. Jameson & S. Musteață, eds., *Transforming Heritage Practice in the 21st Century: Contributions from Community Archaeology*. Cham: Springer, pp. 369–85.

Hesmondhalgh, D. (2008). Towards a critical understanding of music, emotion and self-identity. *Consumption Markets & Culture*, 11(4), 329–43.

Historic England (2014). *Heritage Makes You Happy*. https://historicengland .org.uk/whats-new/news/heritage-makes-you-happy/#:~:text=Research% 20by%20the%20Commission%20for,a%20sense%20of%20civic% 20pride.

Hubbard, P. (1995). Urban design and local economic development: A case study in Birmingham. *Cities*, 12(4), 243–51.

Humphries, G. (2018). *Friday Night at the Oxford*. Woonona: Last Day of School.

Janes, R. R. & Sandell, R. (2019). Posterity has arrived: The necessary emergence of museum activism. In R. R. Janes & R. Sandell, eds., *Museum Activism*. New York: Routledge, pp. 1–21.

Johnston, R. & Marwood, K. (2017). Action heritage: Research, communities, social justice. *International Journal of Heritage Studies*, 23(9), 816–31.

Jordan, J. (2021). Detroit's historic Blue Bird Inn won't be demolished after all. *Detroit Metro Times*, 8 January. www.metrotimes.com/city-slang/archives/ 2021/01/08/detroits-historic-blue-bird-inn-wont-be-demolished-after-all.

Joy, C. (2020). *Heritage Justice*. Cambridge: Cambridge University Press.

Kerr, G., Dombkins, K. & Jelley, S. (2012). 'We love the Gong': A marketing perspective. *Journal of Place Management and Development*, 5(3), 272–9.

Kickstarter (2018). *The Club Heaven Sound System: Restoring a Detroit Legend*. www.kickstarter.com/projects/detroitsound/the-club-heaven-sound-system-restoring-a-detroit-l.

Kinkead, D. (2016). Detroit case study. In D. K. Carter, ed., *Remaking Post-industrial Cities: Lessons from North America and Europe*. New York: Routledge, pp. 46–65.

Klamer, A., Mignosa, A. & Petrova, L. (2013). Cultural heritage policies: A comparative perspective. In I. Rizzo & A. Mignosa, eds., *Handbook on the Economics of Cultural Heritage*. Cheltenham: Edward Elgar, pp. 37–86.

Kozlowski, K. (2021). Detroit's 70-year population decline continues; Duggan says city was undercounted. *The Detroit News*, 12 August. www.detroitnews .com/story/news/local/detroit-city/2021/08/12/census-detroit-population-decline-u-s-census-bureau/5567639001/.

Lawson, C. (2020). Making sense of the ruins: The historiography of deindustrialisation and its continued relevance in neoliberal times. *History Compass*, 18(8), 1–14.

Leonard, M. (2007). Constructing histories through material culture: Popular music, museums and collecting. *Popular Music History*, 2(2), 147–67.

Leonard, M. (2015). The shaping of heritage: Collaborations between independent popular music practitioners and the museum sector. In S. Baker, ed., *Preserving Popular Music Heritage*. London: Routledge, pp. 19–30.

Linkon, S. L. & Russo, J. (2002). *Steeltown USA: Work and Memory in Youngstown*. Lawrence: University Press of Kansas.

Loftman, P. & Nevin, B. (1994). Prestige project developments: Economic renaissance or economic myth? A case study of Birmingham. *Local Economy*, 8(4), 307–25.

Logan, W. (2012). Cultural diversity, cultural heritage and human rights: Towards heritage management as human rights-based cultural practice. *International Journal of Heritage Studies*, 18(3), 231–44.

Long, P., Baker, S., Cantillon, Z., Collins, J. & Nowak, R. (2019). Popular music, community archives and public history online: Cultural justice and the DIY approach to heritage. In J. A. Bastian & A. Flinn, eds., *Community Archives, Community Spaces: Heritage, Memory and Identity*. London: Facet, pp. 97–112.

Long, P., Baker, S., Istvandity, L. & Collins, J. (2017). A labour of love: The affective archives of popular music culture. *Archives and Records*, 38(1), 61–79.

Macdonald, S. (2009). *Difficult Heritage: Negotiating the Nazi Past in Nuremberg and Beyond*. London: Routledge.

Macías, A. (2010). 'Detroit was heavy': Modern jazz, bebop, and African American expressive culture. *The Journal of African American History*, 95(1), 44–70.

Martin, S. (1995). From workshop to meeting place? The Birmingham economy in transition. In R. L. Turner, ed., *From the Old to the New: The UK Economy in Transition*. London: Routledge, pp. 199–217.

McEwan, C., Pollard, J. S. & Henry, N. D. (2008). The non-global city of Birmingham UK: A gateway through time. In M. Price & L. Benton-Short, eds., *Migrants to the Metropolis: The Rise of Immigrant Gateway Cities.* Syracuse: University of Syracuse Press, pp. 128–49.

National Park Service (2019). *Detroit Sound Conservancy Reconnaissance Survey.* http://npshistory.com/publications/srs/detroit-sound-conservancy-rs-2019.pdf.

Pedroni, T. C. (2011). Urban shrinkage as a performance of whiteness: Neoliberal urban restructuring, education, and racial containment in the post-industrial, global niche city. *Discourse: Studies in the Cultural Politics of Education*, 32(2), 203–15.

Pennington, A., Jones, R., Bagnall, A. A., South, J. & Corcoran, R. (2019). *Heritage and Wellbeing: The Impact of Historic Places and Assets on Community Wellbeing – A Scoping Review.* https://whatworkswellbeing.org/wp-content/uploads/2020/01/Heritage-scoping-review-March-2019-1.pdf.

Playford Library (2019). Let's rock. *Facebook*, 29 November. www.facebook.com/104506516625/posts/10156386405346626/?d=n.

Punzalan, R. L. & Caswell, M. (2016). Critical directions for archival approaches to social justice. *Library Quarterly*, 86(1), 25–42.

Reitsamer, R. (2018). Gendered narratives of popular music history and heritage. In S. Baker, C. Strong, L. Istvandity & Z. Cantillon, eds., *The Routledge Companion to Popular Music History and Heritage*. London: Routledge, pp. 26–35.

Roberts, L. & Cohen, S. (2014). Unauthorising popular music heritage: Outline of a critical framework. *International Journal of Heritage Studies*, 20(3), 241–61.

Roberts, L. & Cohen, S. (2015). Unveiling memory: Blue plaques as in/tangible markers of popular music heritage. In S. Cohen, R. Knifton, M. Leonard & L. Roberts, eds., *Sites of Popular Music Heritage: Memories, Histories, Places*. London: Routledge, pp. 221–38.

Rose, G. (1997). Situating knowledges: Positionality, reflexivities and other tactics. *Progress in Human Geography*, 21(3), 305–20.

Ross, A. (1998). *Real Love: In Pursuit of Cultural Justice*. London: Routledge.

Roued-Cunliffe, H. & Copeland, A. (2017). Introduction: What is participatory heritage? In H. Roued-Cunliffe & A. Copeland, eds., *Participatory Heritage*. London: Facet, pp. xv–xxi.

Rugh, J. S. & Massey, D. S. (2010). Racial segregation and the American foreclosure crisis. *American Sociological Review*, 75(5), 629–51.

Ryzewski, K. (2017). Making music in Detroit: Archaeology, popular music, and post-industrial heritage. In L. McAtackney & K. Ryzewski, eds.,

Contemporary Archaeology and the City: Creativity, Ruination, and Political Action. Oxford: Oxford University Press, pp. 69–90.

Ryzewski, K. (2019). Detroit 139: Archaeology and the future-making of a post-industrial city. *Journal of Contemporary Archaeology*, 6(1), 85–100.

Ryzewski, K. (2021). *Detroit Remains: Archaeology and Community Histories of Six Legendary Places*. Tuscaloosa: University of Alabama Press.

Safransky, S. (2018). Land justice as a historical diagnostic: Thinking with Detroit. *Annals of the American Association of Geographers*, 108(2), 499–512.

Schofield, J. & Wright, R. (2021). Sonic heritage, identity and music-making in Sheffield, 'Steel City'. *Heritage & Society*, 13(3), 198–222.

Schultz, J. (1985). *Steel City Blues*. Ringwood: Penguin Books.

Shaw, D. V. (2000). The post-industrial city. In R. Paddison, ed., *Handbook of Urban Studies*. London: Sage, pp. 284–95.

Shaw, K. & Porter, L. (2009). Introduction. In L. Porter & K. Shaw, eds., *Whose Urban Renaissance? An International Comparison of Urban Regeneration Strategies*. New York: Routledge, pp. 1–7.

Simpson, M. (2009). Museums and restorative justice: Heritage, repatriation and cultural education. *Museum International*, 61(1–2), 121–9.

Slager, E. J. (2020). Ruin tours: Performing and consuming decay in Detroit. *Urban Geography*, 41(1), 124–42.

Smith, L. (2006). *Uses of Heritage*. London: Routledge.

Sugrue, T. J. (1996). *The Origins of the Urban Crisis: Race and Inequality in Postwar Detroit*. Princeton: Princeton University Press.

Taçon, P. S. C. & Baker, S. (2019). New and emerging challenges to heritage and well-being: A critical review. *Heritage*, 2(2), 1300–15.

Thibodeau, I. & Noble, B. (2018). Most Detroiters in a decade worked in September. *The Detroit News*, 8 November. www.detroitnews.com/story/business/2018/11/08/labor-statistics-unemployment-rate-detroit-lower/1932604002/.

United States Bureau of Labor Statistics (2021). *Detroit Area Economic Summary*. www.bls.gov/regions/midwest/summary/blssummary_detroit.pdf.

United States Census Bureau (2021). *QuickFacts: Detroit City, Michigan*. www.census.gov/quickfacts/detroitcitymichigan.

van der Hoeven, A. & Brandellero, A. (2015). Places of popular music heritage: The local framing of a global cultural form in Dutch museums and archives. *Poetics*, 51(1), 37–53.

Vawda, S. (2019). Museums and the epistemology of injustice: From colonialism to decoloniality. *Museum International*, 71(1–2), 72–9.

Vecchiola, C. (2006). Detroit's rhythmic resistance: Electronic music and community pride. Unpublished PhD Thesis, University of Michigan. https://deepblue.lib.umich.edu/handle/2027.42/125916.

Vecchiola, C. (2011). Submerge in Detroit: Techno's creative response to urban crisis. *Journal of American Studies*, 45(1), 95–111.

Waitt, G. & Gibson, C. (2009). Creative small cities: Rethinking the creative economy in place. *Urban Studies*, 46(5/6), 1223–46.

Watson, S. (1991). Gilding the smokestacks: The new symbolic representations of deindustrialised regions. *Environment and Planning D: Society and Space*, 9(1), 59–70.

Wayne State University (2021). *SIS Alumna Is on a Mission to Preserve Music History in Detroit*. https://sis.wayne.edu/news/sis-alumna-is-on-a-mission-to-preserve-music-history-in-detroit-42613.

Wheeler, W. (2010). *Steel City Sound*. https://steelcitysound.wordpress.com.

Wheeler, W. (2013a). An update. *Steel City Sound*, 16 March. https://web.archive.org/web/20181117093610/http://www.steelcitysound.net/2013/03/an-update.html.

Wheeler, W. (2013b). Wollongong city gallery exhibition (Dec 2014–Feb 2015). *Steel City Sound*, 6 June. https://web.archive.org/web/20181117093802/http://www.steelcitysound.net/2013/06/wollongong-city-gallery-exhibition-dec.html.

Wilson, C. A. (1992). Restructuring and the growth of concentrated poverty in Detroit. *Urban Affairs Quarterly*, 28(2), 187–205.

Witcomb, A. & Buckley, K. (2013). Engaging with the future of 'critical heritage studies': Looking back in order to look forward. *International Journal of Heritage Studies*, 19(6), 562–78.

Wollongong Art Gallery (2014). *Steel City Sound: 50 Years of Rock 'N Roll in Wollongong*, exhibition catalogue. www.wollongongartgallery.com/exhibitions/Documents/Steel%20City%20Sound%20Exhibition%20Catalogue.pdf.

Zion, L. (1987). The impact of the Beatles on pop music in Australia: 1963–1966. *Popular Music*, 6(3), 291–311.

Zlatopolsky, A. (2017). How Detroit Sound Conservancy helps restore Motor City music history. *Detroit Free Press*. https://eu.freep.com/story/entertainment/music/2017/04/19/detroit-sound-conservancy-music-preservation/100459438/.

Acknowledgements

This research was made possible by funds provided by the Griffith Centre for Social and Cultural Research, the Arts, Education and Law Group at Griffith University, and a Griffith University Senior Deputy Vice Chancellor Special Support Award. Our thanks, in particular, go to Professor Susan Forde, Professor Gerry Docherty and Professor Ned Pankhurst for their belief in the project. We extend our thanks to Lauren Chalk for research assistance with NVivo coding and literature research, and Dr Bob Buttigieg for research assistance in the editing and compiling of the Detroit and Birmingham editions of the *Sounds of Our Town* zines. Thanks, too, to Dr Lauren Istvandity and Professor Paul Long for ongoing scholarly collaborations, including being part of the early workings around the concept of cultural justice. We are so grateful to John Monteleone for allowing us in-kind use of a space at the Wollongong Art Gallery to host our public panel. Our deepest gratitude goes to all the participants in this project who gave their time to be interviewed, who took us on bespoke tours of the case study cities and who contributed to the public panel and project zines. In particular, thank you to Jez Collins of the Birmingham Music Archive and Dr Carleton Gholz of the Detroit Sound Conservancy for being with us every step of the way.

Cambridge Elements ≡

Music and the City

Simon McVeigh

Goldsmiths, University of London

Simon McVeigh is Professor of Music at Goldsmiths, University of London, and President of the Royal Musical Association. His research focuses on British musical life 1700–1945; and on violin music and performance practices of the period. Books include *Concert Life in London from Mozart to Haydn* (Cambridge) and *The Italian Solo Concerto 1700–1760* (Boydell). Current work centres on London concert life around 1900: a substantial article on the London Symphony Orchestra was published in 2013 and a book exploring London's musical life in the Edwardian era is in preparation for Boydell. He is also co-investigator on the digital concert-programme initiative *InConcert*.

Laudan Nooshin

City, University of London

Laudan Nooshin is Professor in Music at City University, London. She has research interests in creative processes in Iranian music; music and youth culture in Iran; urban sound; music in Iranian cinema and music and gender. Her publications include *Iranian Classical Music: The Discourses and Practice of Creativity* (2015, Ashgate, awarded the 2016 British Forum for Ethnomusicology Book Prize); *Music and the Play of Power in the Middle East, North Africa and Central Asia* (ed. 2009, Ashgate) and *The Ethnomusicology of Western Art Music* (ed. 2013, Routledge), as well as numerous journal articles and book chapters. Between 2007 and 2011, Laudan was co-editor of the journal *Ethnomusicology Forum*.

About the Series

Elements in Music and the City sets urban musical cultures within new global and cross-disciplinary perspectives

The series aims to open up new ways of thinking about music in an urban context, embracing the widest diversity of music and sound in cities across the world. Breaking down boundaries between historical and contemporary, and between popular and high art, it seeks to illuminate the diverse urban environment in all its exhilarating and vivid complexity. The urban thus becomes a microcosm of a much messier, yet ultimately much richer, conception of the 'music of everyday life'.

Rigorously peer-reviewed and written by leading scholars in their fields, each Element offers authoritative and challenging approaches towards a fast-developing area of music research. Elements in Music and the City will present extended case-studies within a comparative perspective, while developing pioneering new theoretical frameworks for an emerging field.

The series is inherently cross-disciplinary and global in its perspective, as reflected in the wide-ranging multi-national advisory board. It will encourage a similar diversity of approaches, ranging from the historical and ethnomusicological to contemporary popular music and sound studies.

Written in a clear, engaging style without the need for specialist musical knowledge, *Elements in Music and the City* aims to fill the demand for easily accessible, quality texts available for teaching and research. It will be of interest not only to researchers and students in music and related arts, but also to a broad range of readers intrigued by how we might understand music and sound in its social, cultural and political contexts

Cambridge Elements ≡

Music and the City

Elements in the Series

Printed in the United States
by Baker & Taylor Publisher Services